Praise for *Co*

"A must-read. Author Jeff Kaye is one of a small number of investigative journalists who continue to document — and make discoveries about — the torture of "war on terror" detainees. Despite the massive secrecy that renders FOIA documents black with redactions and gaps in the narrative, he uncovers evidence of the severe abuse of detainees alleged to have committed suicide."

— Martha Davis, Ph.D. Director, *Doctors of the Dark Side* and *Expert Witness: Health Professionals on the Frontline Against Torture*

"Painstakingly and tenaciously researched, this book provides a forensic accounting of the unethical care provided to Guantánamo detainees. This research must be considered a definitive reference for scholars in the field."

— Dr. Remington Nevin, Physician epidemiologist board certified in Public Health and General Preventive Medicine by the ABPM. Expert consultant in antimalarial toxicity

"This is an exemplary dissection of key information obtained by the author through his dogged pursuit of Freedom of Information Act requests. The book raises important questions and makes a strong case for criminal negligence surrounding the deaths in custody of Messrs. Al Hanashi and Al Amri at GITMO. A must-read for anyone interested in the human condition at the Cuban base."

— Professor Almerindo Ojeda, Director, Center for the Study of Human Rights in the Americas, University of California, Davis

"A must read for people who believe in their country when right and seek to make it right when wrong."

— Peter M. Newton, Ph.D., author of *Leadership in Groups*, and *Happiness, A Novel*

Cover-up at Guantanamo

*The NCIS Investigation into the "Suicides" of
Mohammed Al Hanashi and Abdul Rahman Al Amri*

Jeffrey S. Kaye

Text copyright © 2016

Jeffrey S. Kaye

All Rights Reserved

All documents from the Freedom of Information Act (FOIA) request to NCIS, which are the primary materials upon which this book was written, as well as other relevant documents, can be accessed at:

www.GuantanamoTruth.com

* * * *

Cover photo:
Typical Guantanamo cell door in Camp Delta, 2007

Original caption:
"The door of a cell at Camp Delta, Naval Station Guantanamo Bay, Cuba. An opening at the top of the cell lets guards pass things to detainees, and openings at the bottom allow guards to shackle detainees' feet before transporting them."

Original link to photo:
https://commons.wikimedia.org/wiki/File:Guantanamo_celldoor,_Camp_Delta_-_1.jpg
(This image is a work of a U.S. military or Department of Defense employee, taken or made as part of that person's official duties. As a work of the U.S. federal government, the image is in the public domain.)

Every soul will taste death, and you will only be given your [full] compensation on the Day of Resurrection. So he who is drawn away from the Fire and admitted to Paradise has attained [his desire]. And what is the life of this world except the enjoyment of delusion.

Koran 3:185[1]

A dungeon horrible, on all sides round,
As one great furnace flamed; yet from those flames
No light; but rather darkness visible
Served only to discover sights of woe,
Regions of sorrow, doleful shades, where peace
And rest can never dwell, hope never comes
That comes to all, but torture without end
Still urges, and a fiery deluge fed
With ever-burning sulphur unconsumed.
Such place Eternal Justice has prepared
For those rebellious; here their prison ordained
In utter darkness, and their portion set,
As far removed from God and light of Heaven
As from the centre thrice to th' utmost pole.

John Milton, Paradise Lost, Book I, 61-75

"Investigators don't guess, Deputy. They study. They analyze. They make inference based on evidence and facts."

CBS TV show NCIS, "Charade," Season 13, Episode 20[2]

To those imprisoned and tortured in countries around the world, and to those "disappeared"

Table of Contents

Preface and Initial Findings

Chapter 1
Background to an Investigation

Chapter 2
Key Evidence Missing in Guantanamo Detainee's Death: An Inside Look at the Death of Mohammed Al Hanashi

Chapter 3
Al Hanashi's "Testament" and Suicide Note (transcription)

Chapter 4
"The only solution is death": Al Hanashi's Final Days

Chapter 5
The Mysterious Death of Abdul Rahman Al Amri

Chapter 6
Latif, Another Nightmarish Death at Guantanamo

Chapter 7
Concluding Thoughts

Acknowledgments

About the Author

Endnotes

Preface and Initial Findings

This short book presents the findings of a personal investigation into the deaths of two Guantanamo detainees, purportedly by suicide, one during the Presidential reign of George W. Bush, the other during Barack Obama's administration. The conclusion from an examination of the documentary evidence is that the primary investigatory agency at Guantanamo likely covered up the true circumstances of their deaths.

Evidence of a cover-up is drawn from clear evidence of missing, suppressed, and mishandled material, and by examining contradictory testimony from witnesses interviewed by the Naval Criminal Investigative Service (NCIS). There is also to the trained medical eye, evidence of insufficient or inadequate medical procedures, particularly in the treatment of severe mental illness. The matter is made worse when one considers that the mental illness was largely caused by the trauma of indefinite incarceration, abusive conditions of confinement, and the use of torture and cruel, inhumane and degrading treatment during interrogation.

Guantanamo detainees also endured, among other things, isolation, forced feedings, sleep deprivation, constant surveillance, and coerced drugging. All of this was unethical and illegal.

In the case of the deaths of the two detainees – Abdul Rahman Al Amri, who died in 2007, and Mohammed Salih Al Hanashi, who died in 2009 – direct evidence of a crime, via witness testimony or other incriminating prima facie evidence, is lacking. We must rely as prosecutors often do on circumstantial evidence, which is "evidence that proves a fact or event by inference."[3]

The evidence revealed in the pages that follow demonstrates that NCIS conducted at best a shoddy investigation into the deaths of the two detainees. The inadequacy of the investigations – not to mention the ongoing censorship involved in releasing information about these cases – was likely intended to help hide either criminal activities and/or professional negligence, including criminal negligence, by Guantanamo staff, or possibly by other governmental agencies.

In the death of Adnan Latif, which is examined at the close of this book, the U.S. Army investigation into his death determined that Guantanamo staff did not adequately follow camp procedures in matters of detention and safety, including medical procedures, in a way that contributed to Latif's death by suicide (if he did indeed die by suicide).

Latif's death is examined as it is germane to the overall theme of this book, and we shall see that our examination of events will also include important references, and even new revelations, about the deaths at Guantanamo of three other detainees by purported suicide in 2006. Still, what follows in these pages will primarily concern the deaths of Al Hanashi and Al Amri, and the problematic investigation by NCIS into their deaths. Since NCIS is tasked with the primary investigation into detainee deaths at Guantanamo, it made sense to focus on NCIS's activities, as an exemplar of the secretive U.S. government operation at Guantanamo.

The possible criminality and compromised nature of the NCIS investigations is especially highlighted in the case of Al Hanashi, where NCIS was forced in the middle of its death query to open a subordinate investigation – reported for the first time here – into why the Guantanamo computerized detainee database system was ordered turned off as soon as Al Hanashi's body was discovered. Even more suspicious, the order to shut off computer entries apparently was given by an unidentified NCIS agent him or herself!

The results of the NCIS investigation into who ordered the shutdown of the computer documentation of events upon discovery of the body of Al Hanashi has never been revealed. The FOIA office for NCIS has insisted they have sent me all the materials on the subject they have.

The shutdown of the detainee database – known as the Detainee Information Management System, or DIMS – was no small event. The situation surrounding DIMS was so sensitive that no one I approached would speak to me on the record about it.

The DIMS database documented the "Who, What, When, Where, Why, and How"[4] of what went on in Guantanamo's cell blocks and detainee hospital, and could have provided a contemporaneous timeline of events immediately following the discovery of al Hanashi's body, free from the vagaries of memory or dissembling.

The order to turn off the computer data system was not the end of strange activities surrounding the DIMS. Much later, after the investigation was closed, NCIS revealed that the entire record for the day Al Hanashi died – and the following day – had disappeared entirely, *including* portions of the DIMS computer logs that NCIS had documented previously existed. (This will be discussed in greater detail in the narrative that follows.)

The fact that official notification of the missing computer database logs at Guantanamo came only *after* I filed a Freedom of Information Act request with NCIS into its investigation of Al Hanashi's death seems, at least on the surface, suspicious. It suggests that evidence was possibly destroyed after the fact, once deeper journalistic interest in the case was shown.

There are many questions surrounding the death of Al Hanashi. For example, this young prisoner from Yemen, who never met with an attorney, and who was (like Al Amri and Latif) a hunger striker at the U.S. Navy base prison, reportedly strangled himself using an elastic band from his underwear. But the brief-like underwear with elastic bands was *not* the type of underwear military authorities had identified as used by detainees. Where did it come from?

Neither the autopsy report nor the NCIS "Investigative Action" reports mention any discovery of the altered remnants of the undergarments. It says NCIS agents supplied the medical examiners only with a *replica* of the "white brief" issued to the prisoners. The examiners found the ligature on Al Hanashi's neck to be "identical to the elastic band of the examined brief," i.e., to the supposed *replica* of the "white brief" NCIS agents themselves supplied. Authorities implied that the piece of elastic cloth wrapped around Al Hanashi's neck was identical to what he was supposed to be wearing as a prisoner. But that wasn't true.

In the case of Abdul Rahman Al Amri, who supposedly fashioned a noose out of his bed sheet and hanged himself, NCIS and U.S. Army lab technicians made special, detailed efforts to match the suicide materials to the remnants of Al Amri's bed sheet. (As we shall see, there were still problems completing the mutilated bed sheet with the materials of the rope and bindings ostensibly fashioned from it). Yet in the case of Al Hanashi, NCIS seemed indifferent to the question as to what happened to the rest of the underwear from which the ligature that killed him was supposedly derived. It seems to have disappeared.

The mental health of Al Hanashi in the days and weeks leading up to his death, and the treatment he received in Guantanamo's Behavioral Health Unit (BHU) in the detainee hospital, is of clear importance. He made multiple suicide attempts in the weeks prior to his "suicide." Autopsy examiners found his body was covered with many scars. His forehead was riddled with fresh lesions from head banging and from one particularly gruesome suicidal action, when less than a month before he died he deliberately slammed his head into a steel bolt on a wire fence in the detainee's small recreation area. As a result of the bolt incident, he had been placed on suicide watch and forced to wear a special suicide smock for his own protection. Despite his persistent suicidal behavior, and even though a nurse had warned authorities that Al Hanashi was suicidal, he was provided both materials and clothing and possibly time alone without observation to kill himself, if he did indeed kill himself.

Despite his very recent multiple suicide attempts, according to released documents it is unclear if Al Hanashi was on suicide watch on the evening of June 1, 2009, the day he died in a cell in the BHU. His autopsy report states, "[he] has been on a suicide watch at BHU, where he is seen daily by medical staff." As revealed by the NCIS interview with the Senior Medical Officer at the BHU, Al Hanashi was supposedly on a "directed suicide list" drawn up by another detainee, yet it seems no extra safety precautions were being taken at the time at the time of his death.

According to interviews with BHU personnel, Al Hanashi had become obsessed with the deaths of three detainees, supposedly by suicide, three years earlier in June 2006. Reportedly, he felt guilty that he did not die then himself. A few weeks before his own death, he had vaguely formulated plans to meet with one of the BHU nurses to discuss something related to the 2006 "suicides"[5] on the upcoming anniversary of those deaths. The nurse reported this to camp medical officials, as she was supposed to. But within days, or possibly even the next day (the timeline is unclear), Al Hanashi was dead.

The day of Al Hanashi's death, June 1, 2009, was also notable for marking a change in how disciplinary rules were to be enforced in the psychiatric hospital. A turn to harsher discipline consistent with the rest of the camp prison facilities upset Al Hanashi and other detainees in the camp's psychiatric ward, as one guard told NCIS investigators. Moreover, the rules change was the topic of a final conversation between Al Hanashi and the BHU Chief on the day he died.

When in that final meeting Al Hanashi told the Chief he thought Guantanamo authorities were torturing him, the Chief by his own admission turned on his heel and walked immediately away from the startled detainee. We know Al Hanashi was astonished by the Chief's abrupt departure, as he specifically described his upset over this in what appeared to be if not a suicide note, at least the very last thing he ever wrote the evening he died.

"I have heard from the guards that [sic] are going to apply the same rules on us as the other camps," Al Hanashi wrote the day he died, "but when the highest ranking officer in the camp came and talked to me while I was walking he informed me that this camp will have the same rules as the others, and when I asked the help of the psychologist who was present, he said the rules will apply on everybody then he left without saying anything more. Even the officer who was close to him was surprised by his inappropriate behavior as someone who is supposed to be in a humanitarian position. At that time I knew that the only solution is death before they transgress on our religion the way they do in the other camps."

The Chief remembered the incident, too.

"I emphasized to him that even at a hospital there had to be some rules in place," the Chief said in his statement to NCIS. "He then said he felt was [sic] being tortured. This is a normal response to a verbal disagreement between staff and a detainee. In this case, to avoid an argument with [Al Hanashi] I walked away from him without a response. This is what I usually do when a detainee accuses staff of torture."[6]

From this incident we learn a great deal about the inner workings of Guantanamo – that detainees routinely complained about being tortured, and that their medical providers routinely ignored such complaints, disparaging them as derived from routine disagreements between staff and patients, a type of pervasive detainee hysteria about abuse. But everything we have learned about the regime inside Guantanamo shows that the claims of torture, or at least most of them, were true.

As regards this episode, it is also worth noting that Al Hanashi wrote that he met with the "highest ranking officer in the camp." That was likely Guantanamo commander Rear Admiral David M. Thomas, Jr. (Thomas was replaced in June 2009 by Admiral Thomas H. Copeman III.) It's possible, however, that Al Hanashi was referring to the commander of the camp's Joint Detention Group, Colonel Bruce Vargo. Whoever it was, it was extraordinary that the commanding officer at Guantanamo would have discussed the changes in rules in the Behavioral Health Unit with Al Hanashi. But as we shall see, the oft-suicidal prisoner from Yemen was also considered a leader in the camp.

Al Hanashi entered the BHU from Camp 6 in January 2009 for "suicidal ideations," around which time he was caught with a noose he had fashioned. The documents show he was put on suicide watch on at least one occasion. It seems likely he was placed on suicide watch more than that, however. But if on June

1, the day he died, he was on suicide watch, he was not wearing the special suicide smock worn by those typically held in the BHU under special suicide surveillance. The 31-year-old was discovered on the floor of his cell in a fetal position under a blanket, dressed "in khaki shirt and pants without undergarments." According to the autopsy report, the clothes were "general issue of the detention center." Yet, in one guard's statement to NCIS, he was shocked to see the dead Hanashi wearing a tee shirt, as he "was not authorized to wear a tee-shirt so the white fabric around his neck caught my attention."[7]

Other particulars of his death are contradictory, such as how the ligature that killed him was placed and secured. The ligature that strangled Al Hanashi is described by autopsy examiners as having been twisted tight on the left side of his neck, but a witness at the scene told investigators it was twisted tight on the right side. The method of securing the ligature also is somewhat obscure.

Then there is the issue of the "constant video surveillance" inside prisoner cells in Guantanamo. Former Gitmo guard Terry Holdbrooks told attendees at an April 30, 2010 event at the UC Davis Center for the Study of Human Rights in the Americas, "With the monitoring system that was in place just in the poorly constructed camps, let alone Camp 5 and Camp Echo, which are under constant video surveillance, there's no way that a suicide could take place. There was a number of suicide attempts while I was there, but we always caught them."[8]

How could a prisoner under "constant video surveillance" find the time to fashion a suicide apparatus and also strangle himself, providing the crucial minutes needed as well for the hypoxia to kill him?

In November 2009, Guantanamo spokesman Lt. Cmdr. Brook DeWalt told me for an article at Truthout[9] that, while he couldn't comment on whether Al Hanashi had been videotaped in his cell, no Guantanamo detainee goes more than "three minutes" without being checked, one way or another.

The near constant monitoring also tallies with what a prison doctor told journalist Naomi Wolf, who had visited the cells where Al Hanashi had been held on the day or so prior to his death. "They check on prisoners every three minutes," he told her.[10] In addition, Wolf reported, "According to Cortney Busch of Reprieve, a British organization that represents Guantánamo detainees, there is video running on prisoners in the psychiatric ward at all times, and there is a guard posted there continually, too."

The same questions surrounding surveillance of the detainees also arises for the other prisoner whose death we are examining, Abdul Rahman Al Amri – a so-called "high-value" detainee from Saudi Arabia. One wonders how he had the time to construct a rope and noose for himself, secure it to a grating in his cell, and tie his hands behind his back and then hang himself in three minute's time, given the amount of surveillance of his person and his cell. The medical authorities I consulted say it takes at least 3-5 minutes to die when strangling oneself by partial hanging, as Al Amri is assumed to have done.[11] (The heart may go on beating itself for some minutes more, which may be why one corpsman found a pulse on Al Amri still when discovered in his cell.)

How did Al Amri find the time to kill himself unless there was a total breakdown in camp standard operating procedures? Or is there a more sinister explanation?

The case of Al Amri, like Al Hanashi, involves serious problems with the presented evidence. Even as some of those problems are summarized here, it's important to note that the FOIA release of investigatory material on the deceased Saudi prisoner is terribly truncated. Only about 11 percent of all documents, or 63 out of a presumed 584 pages, were handed over in the FOIA release. Much of what was released was horribly redacted. All documents referred to from the FOIA release on Al Hanashi and Al Amri are available online at www.GuantanamoTruth.com.

Still, enough material from the investigation into Al Amri's death was released to see that a guard or medical staff member likely destroyed important evidence. According to interviews with witnesses, it appears that, wittingly or not, a piece of cloth fashioned presumably by Al Amri, or somehow used in his death, was thrown out, possibly with medical trash. While speculative, it is possible this missing piece of sheet was to gag or suffocate the Saudi prisoner. This possibility is explored later in this book.

Whatever happened with the missing cloth, NCIS does not seem to have seriously followed it up. Or maybe they did, but the fact is buried within hundreds of pages of withheld documentation. What we do know from some of the extant documentation is that NCIS investigators at least asked some of the witnesses about it, and we can read the witnesses' disclaimers of any knowledge about what happened. Even so, some of the witnesses tentatively speculate the missing evidence was thrown out in the trash.

In general, in Al Amri's case, laboratory evidence was not fully exploited and leads were not pursued. Important questions appear not to have been asked, such as why Al Amri died with his hands tied behind his back. Nor did NCIS document how a detainee who was heavily monitored by both guards and video camera was able to find the time to create the rope that killed him. Nor could all the pieces of "rope" discovered be accounted for in relation to Al Amri's bed sheet.

Even if there were no problems with how the "rope" was made or where it came from, how did a rope made of material so fragile that tape was needed by investigators to hold it together suffice to carry the weight of a man hanging himself?

The autopsy examiners assumed that altered bed sheets were used for the hanging. But according to a summarized witness statement (pg. 7) by Maj. Gen. (ret.) Mike Dunleavy, who became commander of Guantanamo's interrogation Task Force 170 in February 2002, the sheets used at Guantanamo were "changed" under his order "to the sheets in the federal prison system so they can't be torn or tied."[12]

This fact calls into question the narrative on Al Amri's death, as well as that of the three 2006 Guantanamo "suicides," who were said to have fashioned nooses, in part, out of torn bed sheets. Indeed, nine former British detainees imprisoned and later freed from Guantanamo questioned the 2006 suicides, in part, because they did not have "bed sheets that could easily be constructed into a noose."[13]

Dunleavy's order wasn't the government's only change in bed sheet policy. In a September 6, 2006 memo to the Commander of U.S. Southern Command, the portion of the Pentagon that had jurisdiction over Guantanamo, Joint Task Force Guantanamo Commander Rear Admiral Harry B. Harris, Jr. said, "as a result of the [June] 2006 suicides, bed sheets were issued each night at 2200 and collected each morning at 0500."[14]

Other questions or evidence in the Al Amri case that should have been made available also create doubt about the verdict of suicide. How big were the air vents in the grate to which the rope was allegedly tied? Were they big enough for Al Amri to "snake a torn sheet through it to anchor" the rope?[15] Presumably there were pictures taken of the cell and the air vent grating, but none of those have been publicly released.

Maybe there's no picture of the grating because it would be obvious it was unusable. Australian David Hicks, who spent a good deal of time in Camp 5, and found it a place for which it was impossible to plan a successful suicide, described the grating in his cell as 30 centimeters square. It was made up of "many little holes."[16]

These questions of instrumentality are not the end of the mystery. The toxicology report on Al Amri showed he was tested after his death for the presence of two antimalarial drugs, chloroquine and mefloquine. Autopsy doctors uniquely singled out the testing for mefloquine, as if it were something special that needed to be tested. While unusual, this was not a unique case, as one of the three 2006 detainees "suicides" was also tested for mefloquine.

This was strange as there was no reason to believe that the drug mefloquine was ever taken by or applied to Al Amri or any other detainee after their initial in-processing at Guantanamo. The fact that standard operating procedures called for initial dosing for all detainees of full treatment doses of mefloquine was controversial enough, as described in the next chapter below. But why would a prisoner, held for years at the

Cuban base, where no cases of malaria transmission have ever been reported, have to be tested after a supposed suicide for the presence of an antimalarial drug?

The inference is that some kind of medical experiment was being run. We already know, from the U.S. Senate Church Committee investigations of the 1970s that the CIA stockpiled the antimalarial drug cinchonine as an "incapacitating agent."[17] Were the side effects of mefloquine – a drug chemically similar to cinchonine – or even chloroquine, used to incapacitate or disorient prisoners, or were experiments run on this? Al Amri's death and the toxicology investigation into whether he had levels of mefloquine in his blood demand some kind of answer.[18]

Mefloquine side effects can be serious, ranging from anxiety and dizziness, to depression and psychosis. Some people are more susceptible to its effects than others. What better way to determine the differential effects of the drug than to administer to an entire population the medication and see how they react? The mass administration of mefloquine was Standard Operating Procedure for all new detainees at Guantanamo. Were Al Amri and other one of the 2006 "suicides," Ali Abdullah Ahmed, who was tested after his death for the presence of mefloquine, discovered to be more vulnerable to mefloquine side effects? Was the drug used in their interrogations, and was that why it was queried in the toxicology studies on only these two detainees and no other deceased detainees? If there were the presence or ongoing threat of malaria in the camps, where's the evidence for that?

In his book on the NCIS investigation into the 2006 detainee "suicides," Murder in Camp Delta, former Guantanamo guard Joseph Hickman hypothesized that use of mefloquine was part of a "special access program" (SAP) used to experiment with new interrogation (torture) procedures on prisoners. As such, any use of these procedures, including any deaths resulting from them, would be kept secret at top levels of classification. Hickman thought such secrecy might explain why NCIS ran such tainted investigations into the 2006 Guantanamo "suicides."[19] Could the same have been true for Al Amri, or any of the other detainees who died ostensibly by their own hand?

Yet the reader may demand, at this point, some proof that even the idea of medical experiments being undertaken has any probability. Recently I came across just such circumstantial evidence in a report on alleged collaboration between the American Psychological Association (APA) and the Department of Defense and intelligence agencies with regards to post-9/11 interrogation policies that relied on torture and/or cruel treatment of prisoners. The primary author of the report, paid for by APA, was David Hoffman from the Sidley Austin law firm.[20]

According to the report, in 2003 members of the APA, consulting with an "unclassified advisory group" for the Department of Homeland Security's Science and Technology Behavioral Research Program, discussed the possibility of using "Guantanamo Bay subjects as data."[21]

Interestingly, a group composed of mostly military psychologists and some former APA officials, have released a series of formerly inaccessible private emails on their website, some of which are germane to the issue of research on detainees. In one of their releases, Centra Technologies, Inc. analyst Michael Kabrin writes to CIA contractor and RAND researcher Scott Gerwehr regarding questions Gerwehr had about "detainees and D&D."[22] "D&D" stands here, I believe, for "Denial and Deception," and is a term used in the intelligence community to describe intelligence community techniques in relation to the use of secrecy and deception.[23]

Kabrin wrote to Gerwehr on December 7, 2004 (ellipses in original): "As for your question regarding detainees and D&D… I think the sponsor is leaning more toward the 'strategic' D&D operations being carried out. Whatever thoughts and information you have to share would be great. I realize it's a bit difficult to get data on detainees without being read in, so it might be useful to give your thoughts on tactical techniques as well."

By "read in," Kabrin is likely speaking to levels of classified access that allows only those with a "need to know" to be able to get information that is otherwise classified under Special Access Program or other secrecy protocols. Officials at Centra Technologies, for instance, were likely "read in" to the military and CIA's interrogation research program. A Vice News report by Jason Leopold in July 2015[24] revealed that the CIA paid Centra $40 million dollars to help it with "administrative support and other tasks" related to the Senate Intelligence Committee's investigation into the CIA's interrogation and rendition program. The 2004 Kabrin email strongly suggests that Kabrin and Centra employees were "read in" to aspects of research upon detainees that were of interest to RAND counterterrorism researcher Gerwehr.

Whatever the case with Centra, this was not the only time researchers discussed the possible research use of detainees who might not have adequate Geneva protections against being used in experiments, like the prisoners at Guantanamo. A National Research Council meeting in 2008 expressed concern about ethical protections for just such prisoners, who could be used as experimental human subjects without their consent. But they considered a further look into such matters as "beyond the scope" of their inquiry. Interestingly, Hoffman would conclude much the same about possible research on detainees in his own investigation, i.e., such questions went beyond the bounds of his contracted investigation. But I believe I've made my point here: it is not unreasonable to conclude that experiments were conducted at Guantanamo and other U.S. military or intelligence sites that held detainees, and others have raised the issue as well.[25]

Towards the end of this book there is a chapter on the military's investigation into the September 2013 death at Guantanamo, also purportedly by suicide, of Yemeni detainee Adnan Farhan Abd Al Latif. This was the Army's AR 15-6 investigation into Latif's death, and should not be confused with any investigation conducted by NCIS.

Like Al Hanashi, Al Latif had a long history of mental disturbance and suicidal ideation. He was found dead in his cell at Guantanamo's BHU. I never filed a FOIA for the NCIS investigation into Al Latif's death and my account is based primarily on the military's AR 15-6 report on his death, a FOIA request for which was filed initially by reporter Jason Leopold. As I've already noted above, the circumstances of Al Latif's death are pertinent to the themes raised in the deaths of the 2006 detainees, Al Amri in 2007, and Al Hanashi in 2009.

There have been other deaths at Guantanamo, as well, one of which was an Afghan called Inayatullah, also known as Hajji Nassim, who supposedly killed himself in May 2011. Nassim reportedly also suffered from mental illness and spent time in Guantanamo's psychiatric ward. In February of the same year, another Afghan, Awal Gul, a purported former Taliban commander, supposedly died of a heart attack. Much earlier, in December 2007, Afghan detainee Abdul Razzak Hekmati reportedly died of colorectal cancer in Guantanamo.[26]

I have not looked at their deaths in any detail, but suffice it to say that given the poor record of providing transparency or truth by Guantanamo officials, or the government agencies investigating them, we must take the official stories about these deaths with a grain of salt.

It's not impossible there were even more deaths at Guantanamo. At a February 19, 2002 meeting of the Armed Forces Epidemiological Board (AFEB), Captain Alan "Jeff" Yund, a preventive medicine doctor and the Navy's liaison officer to the AFEB, discussed "mortuary affairs" at Guantanamo, part of a larger discussion on health issues at the new prison facility. He told the assembled medical officials, "[a] number of the detainees have died of the wounds that they arrived with" at Guantanamo.[27]

During the meeting, Captain Yund identified himself as working directly with Admiral Steven Hart, the Director of Navy Medicine Research and Development, as well as "a number of other admirals." Yund told me in December 2010 by email that he could not remember the time or place of the event where he was told of the deaths, but said it was "a detailed and fascinating account" of "events and issues" at Guantanamo. He thought he heard about the deaths from a presentation by Captain Al Shimkus, the commanding officer of the U.S. Naval Hospital in Guantanamo Bay in 2002.

Capt. Shimkus was also – though Capt. Yund evidently did not know this – the man who signed off on the mefloquine protocol as part of the in-processing standard operating procedures for new detainees at Guantanamo. In an interview with me for Truthout, Capt. Shimkus said he was told by unnamed officials back in 2002 not to discuss the mefloquine policy.[28] He also denied that he knew anything about any deaths in Guantanamo as discussed by Captain Yund.

I filed a FOIA request to the Guantanamo Naval Hospital regarding "mortuary affairs" on the issue of detainee deaths in the early weeks and months after Guantanamo was opened to "war on terror" prisoners. While the issue bounced around a lot between different departments, in the end I was told there were no documents responsive to my request. I have not been able, due to time constraints, to follow up more.

* * * *

This book contends there was a cover-up by investigative agencies, primarily the NCIS, in regards to the deaths of at least two Guantanamo detainees. This seems a plausible conclusion from the facts presented, and moreover, seems to me more reasonable than other possible conclusions. Of course, there are other possible interpretations. The facts presented could represent merely accidental or chance findings, or represent evidence of simple, i.e., not criminal, negligence or ineptitude on the part of authorities. In the end, the reader will have to decide. To guard against charges of bias, I have heavily footnoted my facts and have either linked to or personally published all relevant documents.

Whatever one believes about these deaths, I believe most will find the censorship involved in these cases by the government to be atrocious. As of the date of writing, outstanding FOIA requests for the U.S. Southern Command AR 15-6 investigations into the deaths of Al Hanashi and Al Amri are still awaiting completion. A SOUTHCOM FOIA officer told me in March 2016 that the reports have been sent to the Office of the Secretary of Defense for final clearance. But approximately six months later I still have not received anything.

As a matter of convergent validity, my analysis of the investigation into the deaths at Guantanamo are consistent with Joe Hickman's presentation, mentioned above and at various times in this book, and with the investigation of Seton Hall Law

School researchers[29] who found numerous serious issues with the NCIS investigation into the deaths of the 2006 detainees, Yasser Talal Al-Zahrani, Mani Shaman Al-Utaybi, and Ali Abdullah Ahmed (aka Salah Ahmed Al-Salami).

The following narrative will describe facts about the deaths of two Guantanamo detainees that have never been presented in public before. The information relies primarily on documents I obtained by Freedom of Information Act request from NCIS regarding their investigation into the deaths of Al Hanashi and Al Amri. All documents from the FOIA I filed with NCIS are being made available online at www.GuantanamoTruth.com.

Because of the vagaries of spelling and transliteration of Arabic names, not to mention possible use of cover names, or on occasion just confusion over names, sometimes in the quotes from documentary material the names of the detainees, and sometimes others, like Osama bin Ladin, are spelled differently. There are different spellings, for instance, of "Mohammed" and "Saleh/Salih." In the case of Abdul Rahman Al Amri, the NCIS investigators routinely used the spelling "Al Umari" for Al Amri. I have kept all quoted spellings as in the original documents. I have continued to use the spelling "Al Amri" myself when I am writing about this detainee, as that is how he was usually referred to in the press.

Chapter 1
Background to an Investigation

Montgomery Street is located in the heart of San Francisco's Financial District, an amalgam of steel and glass skyscrapers and older brick or stucco buildings from the early 20th century, festooned with marble facings, ceramic clay sculptures, art deco frescos, beaux-arts Greek columns, and Italian Renaissance splendor. The skyscrapers there are anchored over old bay mud fill and the wrecks of hundreds of sailing ships abandoned in the rush from prospectors to get to the California gold fields in 1849-50. The famous ferry terminal with its commuters and lunchtime crowds is only a five-minute walk away.

Located on one of the upper floors of the Financial District's newer buildings, far above the intense traffic and the hustle of the chic San Francisco crowds – not to mention 3,078 miles from the Guantanamo Bay Detention Camp – is a jail run by the Department of Homeland Security. Its prisoners are transient, shipped in from detention centers as far as a hundred or more miles away, from jails in scattered depressed towns in California's sweltering Central Valley.

I had been called to meet with one of the prisoners, a young man from a Middle Eastern country, who had been taken in shackles to San Francisco so I could conduct a psychological examination upon him. His immigration attorney wanted to see if his client's claims of torture could be documented, so he could buttress the man's claims of persecution in his home country, hoping to win for the man his petition for political asylum in the United States whenever his case came before an immigration agent or magistrate. He is lucky to have an attorney, for without one he might languish for years in immigration detention, or be peremptorily sent back to the country from which he fled.

The Clinical Director of Survivors International (SI), Uwe Jacobs, had cajoled me into taking on this man's evaluation. Survivors International was a torture treatment center in San Francisco that provided clinical and forensic services to clients seeking asylum. Jacobs, who helped write the famous Istanbul Protocol, a manual on the investigation and documentation of torture, was very good at convincing SI's volunteer clinicians to take on even the most difficult cases. Still, there were usually too many cases and not enough clinicians for them all. (SI has since lost its funding and independent existence, and been folded into county services for immigrants.)

As typical when first approached, I was initially reluctant. In part because such evaluations paid poorly, but inwardly I knew that wasn't the real reason. In fact, it felt good to see I was helping people in special need. My reluctance was emotional and psychological. I knew that these cases took a psychic toll. In order to assess and document the psychological and emotional injury incurred from torture, you had to enter deeply into the subject's personal and subjective experience of that torture. It wasn't enough to ask if one were beaten or sexually abused, you had to ask where and when and how and what it felt like.

The process had an odd resemblance to interrogation, and when I worked with people on such examinations, I went out of my way to explain how the psychological evaluation was different than an interrogation. This was important, as police, military or security and intelligence forces, many of them in countries with alliances to the United States, had interrogated – and tortured – many of them.

"You can stop this interview any time you like," I'd say. "You don't have to answer any question you don't want. You can go to the bathroom or step outside for a smoke anytime you want. You *are* in control."

But this day, I couldn't say that. My "client" was not in control at all. He was dressed in prison garb. He was thousands of miles from home, and watched over by armed guards who sat right outside the glass booth where he, a translator, and I had been guided to conduct the interview.

There was a strange silence to the facility. I didn't see any other prisoners. It was odd that outside this building the financial elite and their lawyers and office workers walked by oblivious to the drama unfolding some stories above them, just as they likely never noticed the tortured who walked among them. Men and women from Africa, Asia, Latin America, and even Europe, of all ages, dressed in cheap clothes, hobbling from injuries, bent over from whippings and from suspensions by arms for hours on end, raped or beaten, with crushed souls and smashed teeth, all walking by to appointments with immigration attorneys, with Homeland Security Courts, with psychologists like me!

I never started out an interview with a subject by soliciting the ostensibly traumatic material. I asked first about their upbringing, family, schooling, relationships, dreams for one's future. When the time came to talk about his or her arrest and torture, I asked if he or she wanted to take a break first. Usually the examinee declined, and we proceeded. Better to get it over with, I presumed they thought. The torture victims I examined usually looked incredibly tense, as if they were braced for an assault.

The man, who appeared before me like a human wreck, had scars on his forehead (like Mohammed Al Hanashi, the man whose life and death occupies the two chapters of this book) from banging his head against stone prison walls. The man's frame was bent like a twig and he sat hunched over. His breathing was labored. His eyes darted from the interpreter to me, over to the guards, at the clock, at the table. It was like he could not be still.

Issues of confidentiality intrude here. I will not identify more this person, nor talk about his tale of torture. I am bound by the ethics of my field, even if it is to the detriment of torture victims in general, whose stories so desperately need to be heard.

But my reactions are not confidential. With this man, as with so many others, I first recoiled in disbelief. What he was telling me could not be true. He must have been making it all up!

I could feel myself *wanting* to disbelieve. I was angry with him, angry at his attorney for setting up the interview, angry at my good friend Uwe for seducing me into this ridiculous and painful charade in a jail I never knew existed only blocks from my small but comfortable Nob Hill office. The intolerable interior psychic pain from the prisoner cascaded off him like penetrating waves of agony. They broke through my denial, which itself was a defense against traumatic exposure. It was true. His story was credible. His symptoms were consistent with his story. His physiological reactions were involuntary and unfeigned. I wrote notes furiously down on yellow legal foolscap. I kept looking up to make eye contact, knowing that I had to keep a connection with this man if I were to get his full story.

Something more happened during my examination, something I cannot write down, out of respect for this man's privacy. But it impressed me more than words could probably say anyway. His pain and humiliation were intense. He was hopeless, and his hopelessness washed over and through me like a sudden release of floodwaters. Conversely, I felt like I was socked in the jaw. I was staggered inwardly.

At the end, the young man was taken away from the glass booth. It was time for me to leave and return to my regular world. He would go back to his cell and wait until later, when a bus would take him and other prisoners back to their detention facility leased in some remote community by immigration services. It would be years before I'd know what happened to him, and I was relieved to hear he'd been finally released from custody.

After the interview, I walked back up California Street to my office, climbing the steep hill that always winded me. A cable car filled with tourists clattered by. But my mind was racing. I don't think I'd ever seen anyone in that much pain before. Or maybe I had, but my denial and other psychological defenses had protected me. This time the defenses were not enough.

I would have to take some kind of action. I felt a sense of commitment that I'd never felt before. What had been an interest in helping others, an intellectual aversion to torture and abuse, and political opposition to the policies of the Bush administration that sanctioned torture, was transmuted into a burning wish to bring the torturers of the world to justice. Only after even more years would I realize that the grandiosity of such a wish was itself a kind of defense against the insane whirlwind of intolerable pain and experiences of the soul beyond the capacity to feel.

Eight years after the election that ended the Bush/Cheney regime, torture still makes the news sometimes. It can still rise to the level of national scandal, as when in December 2014, the Senate Select Committee on Intelligence released their censored version of the Executive Summary of their report on CIA torture.[30] But the actual experiences of the tortured *from their point of view* are seldom part of the national discussion. Exceptions include the release of interviews gathered by the International Committee of the Red Cross of "high-value detainees" held in the CIA's detention and rendition program, published in April 2009 by Mark Danner in the New York Review of Books[31].

There have also been a few books written by former prisoners at Guantanamo, such as Murat Kuranz[32], Moazzam Begg[33], and Mamdouh Habib.[34] One prisoner, Australian David Hicks, wrote his story about torture and imprisonment at Guantanamo, but amazingly the book, Guantanamo: My Journey, was never published in the United States. Other books, like Habib's, are out of print and ridiculously expensive to purchase used.

One important book managed to make it through the U.S. government's attempts to suppress the voices of the tortured. In 2015, human rights activist Larry Siems helped get the Guantanamo diary of Mohamedou Ould Slahi published by Little, Brown.[35] Excerpts from the diary, still heavily censored, a record of Slahi's torture by U.S. forces in Afghanistan and in

Guantanamo, were published in major papers around the world. It was an important break in the wall of silence that accompanies the record of U.S. torture. But as I write this preface, Slahi remains in prison at Guantanamo.

Also as I write this preface (June 2016), some stories of those tortured by U.S. forces are still leaking out. In an Al Jazeera article published a few months ago, prisoners tortured by the CIA in their black site "enhanced interrogation" torture program related their personal tales of abuse.[36] Stories like this are gathered by brave journalists, mostly outside the United States, though there have been some notable domestic exceptions.[37]

The short book that follows concerns the investigation into the death of two Guantanamo detainees. They were not necessarily the most well-known, prisoners, or the most important, if any man's life can be said to be more or less important than another's. They died in circumstances that were suspicious. Like almost all the deaths at the U.S. interrogation and detention center at the U.S. naval base at Guantanamo, their deaths were attributed to suicide.

According to reports from investigators and the Defense Department itself, there have been many suicide attempts at Guantanamo since it opened. A February 2006 report by five UN special rapporteurs, working for the Commission on Human Rights, described the regime of torture and abuse that was seriously impacting the mental health of prisoners:

"Reports indicate that the treatment of detainees since their arrests, and the conditions of their confinement, have had profound effects on the mental health of many of them. The treatment and conditions include the capture and transfer of detainees to an undisclosed overseas location, sensory deprivation and other abusive treatment during transfer; detention in cages without proper sanitation and exposure to extreme temperatures; minimal exercise and hygiene; systematic use of coercive interrogation techniques; long periods of solitary confinement; cultural and religious harassment; denial of or severely delayed communication with family; and the uncertainty generated by the indeterminate nature of confinement and denial of access to independent tribunals. These conditions have led in some instances to serious mental illness, over 350 acts of self-harm in 2003 alone, individual and mass suicide attempts and widespread, prolonged hunger strikes. The severe mental health consequences are likely to be long term in many cases, creating health burdens on detainees and their families for years to come."[38]

The UN investigation inspired a report in April 2007 from Amnesty International, USA: Cruel and Inhuman: Conditions of isolation for detainees at Guantánamo Bay.[39] The report maintained the regime at Guantanamo was even more abusive than in earlier years. The organization lambasted the U.S. government for disregarding "the severe psychological impact on detainees of indefinite confinement."

The first completed suicides at Guantanamo were said to be the deaths of three detainees on June 1, 2006. The Guantanamo commander at the time, Rear Adm. Harry B. Harris Jr., called the purported suicides "asymmetrical warfare waged against us."[40]

The deceased were two Saudi Arabian detainees, Yasser Talal Al-Zahrani and Mani Shaman Al-Utaybi, and third man, Ali Abdullah Ahmed, who was from Yemen. Al Zahrani was only 22 years old, and had been one of the teenagers rendered and imprisoned at the island prison. All had been at one time or another hunger strikers in protest of the draconian regime and indefinite detention. Their presumed suicides were now portrayed as acts of guerilla warfare.

Yet it seemed to some that a planned, exquisitely-timed mass suicide was always highly implausible, particularly in the high-security setting that is Guantanamo. A guard on duty outside the camp where the bodies were found, Joseph Hickman, told Scott Horton at Harper's magazine[41] that the deaths were likely linked to a secret, most likely CIA, black site hidden on the Guantanamo base. As a tower guard, the night of the "suicides" he had witnessed detainees secretly taken out of camp earlier that evening and driven in the direction of the black site.

At the same time, investigators at Seton Hall University Law School's Center for Policy and Research were documenting serious inconsistencies and problems with the official government investigations into the deaths, undertaken by the Naval Criminal Investigative Service (NCIS), the Criminal Investigation Task Force (CITF), U.S. Southern Command, and the Staff Judge Advocates Office (SJA).

The Seton Hall law center issued a comprehensive report on their findings in December 2009.[42] They found the investigations to be incompetent, raising far more questions than they answered. Even more, they complained, as I do in this book, that much of the documentation was redacted.

The Seton Hall investigators ridiculed the claims of a coordinated suicide event. Their reasoning is important for the purposes of the investigation undertaken in this book, and in particular as regards claims made about the actions of Mohammad Al Hanashi prior to his death, as we shall see later.

The 2009 Seton Hall report explains, "There are no documents, statements, video surveillances, log-book notes, DIMS reports, or other records that suggests a coordinated act. No guard was questioned about how the detainees could have communicated to conspire or coordinate their elaborate acts while under constant surveillance." So much for "asymmetrical warfare."

The lack of incriminating DIMS reports was an issue that was to arise again when I received in 2015 the FOIA release of the NCIS report into the death of Yemeni detainee Mohammad Al Hanashi in June 2009. DIMS was an acronym for the Detainee Information Management System, a computer database that was supposed to cover in-depth all actions and interactions, movements, etc. of detainees at Guantanamo. From the first deaths at Guantanamo to the last, the failure of the DIMS system, and in at least one case, the deliberate interference with its operations, was a signal finding of my investigations.

But what *was* the truth about the 2006 "suicides"? Hickman, the guard in the watchtower, wondered about that as well. He had witnessed the warden at the Guantanamo prison facility, Army Colonel Michael Bumgarner, tell prison personnel the day after the deaths that despite the fact it was known in the camp that the prisoners had died with rags stuffed down their throats, they were to say nothing to the press when the Guantanamo authorities told the press the detainees supposedly had hanged themselves. A cover-up was in the making.

In fact, a year after the Harper's article that broke the Hickman account, Almerindo Ojeda, a researcher at University of California, Davis, made a strong case that the three detainees had been killed by a torture technique known as "dryboarding."[43] According to Ojeda, "dryboarding" consists of a form of "controlled suffocation," where a detainee's mouth is stuffed with cloth, and the mouth then taped over with duct tape. (Such a procedure actually happened to Ali Saleh al-Marri, held as an "enemy combatant" in the U.S. Navy brig in Charleston, South Carolina. Al Marri was later sentenced to a U.S. high security prison, and then released and returned to Qatar in January 2015.)

This book raises the possibility that Al Amri in 2007 also was a victim of "dryboarding." Al Amri's case is quite similar to those of the 2006 "suicides." He was found hanging. His hands were bound. He had been a hunger striker. He was tested after his death for the presence of antimalarial medication. A missing piece of cloth from the death scene, reported to investigators and supposedly thrown away with medical trash, could have been used to gag his mouth in an application of the "dryboarding" technique.

Hickman knew the official story of the 2006 "suicides" did not hold together. After leaving his tour of duty at Guantanamo, he tried to put the nightmare of the camp out of his mind, but when a year later another detainee, Abdul Rahman al-Amri, died a supposed suicide, Hickman knew he could not let the story rest. (Al-Amri's death also had an emotional effect upon another important Guantanamo researcher, Andy Worthington.[44]) Hickman began a private investigation into what occurred, later linking up with the Seton Hall researchers led by attorney Mark Denbeaux, who had been an attorney for some Guantanamo detainees. Together, they released a number of reports deconstructing and refuting the official story.

In January 2015, Hickman released a book summarizing his investigation into the 2006 deaths. Murder at Camp Delta: A Staff Sergeant's Pursuit of the Truth About Guantanamo Bay, published by Simon and Schuster, made a big splash in the press. I was hopeful that the issue of the many mysterious deaths at Guantanamo was going to be taken up in a big way. I imagined Congressional hearings, in the midst of a classic newshound race to get the big story, to get the *truth*. None of that happened. At the end of this book, we'll try and understand why the issue of the deaths at Guantanamo has not gained more traction. Certainly one reason to write this book is to spur a further search for both truth and accountability.

In his book, Hickman described his investigation, and concluded that NCIS had suppressed evidence from their report, removed witness statements, failed to interview other crucial witnesses, and in general had produced, at best, shoddy work. At worst, the problems with the NCIS report were circumstantial evidence of a major government cover-up.

Incredibly, one of Hickman's findings concerned a DIMS entry made at 11:43 PM the night the detainees died. It was the only entry "for the entire day of June 9." The entry showed a guard had failed to find the detainees "present." They were only "accounted for." In military language, this meant they probably were not in their cells. Hickman's story about the nighttime trip of the detainees to the CIA black site on base, nicknamed "Camp No," seemed to have documentary backing.

Some years later, when other evidence was being gathered on the deaths of Al Hanashi, and even a later Guantanamo death, that of Adnan Farhan Abd Al Latif in September 2012, DIMS entries were notably missing or never made. As the next chapter of this book will show, in one case the DIMS material went missing only *after* my FOIA on the al Hanashi NCIS investigation was filed! (The FOIA release on Al Amri is so heavily censored, we cannot tell what role DIMS played or didn't play in the investigation of his death.)

Like Hickman and the Seton Hall researchers, I've discovered misplaced documentation, censorship, shoddy forensic work, and even what appears to be evidence tampering in the NCIS investigations into the two deaths I decided to examine. Moreover, this work has proceeded under a general political atmosphere of indifference to the fate of the detainees.

Nearly eight years since President Obama announced he would close Guantanamo, the facility remains open. Its depopulation continues, even as plans to upgrade the facility are also put in place. No one knows what a new president will do, but one thing seems sadly likely: no renunciation of Obama's policy of foregoing intensive further investigation or prosecutions of individuals responsible for torture will take place.

But Guantanamo was never the entire story of the U.S. torture program, and neither were the CIA "black sites" or use of waterboarding.

In November 2014, the United Nations Committee Against Torture (UNCAT) released their "Concluding observations on the third to fifth periodic reports of United States of America"[45] in regards to U.S. adherence to the prohibitions against torture and cruel, inhumane, and degrading forms of treatment of prisoners.

In particular, the committee took aim at the presence of ill-treatment and torture within the Army Field Manual's Appendix M, which purports to describe a "restricted interrogation technique" called "Separation." In a victory for those who oppose government-sanctioned torture and abuse of prisoners, the UNCAT called for the U.S. "to review Appendix M of the Army Field Manual in light of its obligations under the Convention."

More specifically, UNCAT identified the "minimal" sleep regulations in the manual as actually a form of sleep deprivation — "a form of ill-treatment" — and called for adherence to humane norms. In addition, the committee called for the elimination of sensory deprivation in the "field expedient" section of Appendix M, as such sensory deprivation can "create a state of psychosis with the detainee, raising concerns of torture and ill-treatment."

In regards to the military's regime at Guantanamo, UNCAT forcefully said "force-feeding of prisoners on hunger strike constitutes ill-treatment in violation of the Convention." The committee called for the immediate release of all uncharged or cleared detainees, an end to force-feeding and indefinite detention, and investigation of all torture, abuse or ill-treatment charges, including prosecution of those responsible and redress to victims.

The U.S. denied all the UNCAT charges, but exposure of ongoing torture practices allowed by U.S. interrogation instructions continues.[46] Meanwhile, interest in the deaths of various Guantanamo detainees languishes, the interest in Hickman's book notwithstanding. In addition, investigations into the deaths, when not ignored, have been subject to attack in the press.[47]

But mostly there has been neglect. Even when I revealed that the detainee al-Amri had been discovered in his high-security cell in May 2007 dead, suspended with his hands tied behind his back, not one news source picked up the part about the bound hands. A suspicious death at Guantanamo may have been old news already. Another atrocity in a far-away place that the supposedly liberal President of the United States told us we were already trying to move past.

Maybe he was right. Maybe old questions, if not old crimes, are the stuff of dyspeptic cranks and pajama-bedraggled bloggers. Maybe, but I don't think so.

Chapter 2
Key Evidence Missing in Guantanamo Detainee's Death: An Inside Look at the Death of Mohammed Al Hanashi

It's been more than 14 years since the U.S. government started incarcerating "war on terror" prisoners at specially built facilities at the Naval base at Guantanamo Bay. The Cuba-sited camp was chosen precisely to keep operations there as secret and unaccountable as possible.[48] What happens inside the facility is carefully hidden from public view, and this is especially true when prisoners have died.

Officially, the fifth person to die at Guantanamo was a Yemeni prisoner, Mohammed Saleh Al Hanashi. Ruled a death by suicide by authorities, newly released government documents from the investigation into his 2009 death reveal tampering with documentary evidence at the scene, calling into question the legitimacy of the investigation into how he died.

The NCIS materials, which are at times heavily censored, discuss other irregularities with the investigation, including the failure to properly maintain the security of evidence central to a verdict of suicide, which was sent by mail for laboratory analysis.

According to a partial Freedom of Information Act release from the Naval Criminal Investigative Service, or NCIS, into their investigation into the death of Al Hanashi on June 1,

2009, key evidence from a computer detainee tracking and database system was ordered suppressed in the very first minutes after his body was discovered.

According to the FOIA release, an unidentified NCIS agent told Guantanamo staff to turn off the computer database, known as the Detainee Information Management System (DIMS), which monitors all interactions with detainees soon after Hanashi's body was discovered. The question of who ordered this became the object of an investigation that has never been revealed until now.

As NCIS agents discovered that the order came from someone within NCIS itself, an internal investigation was begun to discover why this violation of standard operating procedure took place. No final conclusion concerning this investigation was part of the FOIA release, and while NCIS's FOIA office said all materials were in fact released, NCIS Public Affairs failed to return multiple requests for further comment about the shutdown of DIMS.

Even further cover-up may have taken place later in relation to the computer database files. Nearly 8 months after this author filed a FOIA request on the investigation into Al Hanashi's death, a July 23, 2012 NCIS memo titled "Missing Material from Dossier" found "[a]fter an exhaustive search of all sources" that all the DIMS logs from the Behavioral Health Unit (BHU) for the day of and the day after Al Hanashi's death were "missing and unrecoverable."

Yet some of those logs – those entered *before* the mysterious order to turn off the system – existed because they were quoted in investigative reports in the early days of the NCIS investigation, as will be examined below. The missing logs may have included the identity of the person who ordered the DIMS entry turned off, but we will likely never know who that was now.

A Pattern of Suppressing Evidence?

A similar failure to document key entries into DIMS during the crucial period surrounding a detainee's death took place during the hours surrounding the September 2012 death of another detainee, Adnan Farhan Abd Latif, who like Al Hanashi also died in the Behavioral Health Unit at Guantanamo. A special Army investigation,[49] known as an AR 15-6 report, cited the failure to make entries into the DIMS record at the time of Latif's death as a violation of camp standard operating procedures.

The Army report said, "... the lack of entries did make it difficult after the fact to re-create the immediate events leading up to the point that the guards found [Latif] unresponsive."

Is there a pattern to suppress information from Guantanamo's computer surveillance and database system in instances of detainee deaths?

DIMS is a facility-wide computer logging system used by guards and other Guantanamo personnel to keep copious and detailed notes on every prisoner at the Cuba-based facility.

The DIMS system goes back to the early years of the Guantanamo prison. According to a February 17, 2005 statement by then-commander of Joint Task Force Guantanamo, Army Brig. Gen. Jay Hood, the DIMS system "allows us to keep track of nearly every aspect of a detainee's daily life."[50]

The Army report on Latif's death explained, DIMS "is the primary tool used to track day-to-day information about detainees, and is made up of electronic entries regarding each detainee." Army investigators looking into the Latif case relied on the veracity of DIMS entries as being more reliable than eyewitness memories.[51]

Army investigators had much the same to say regarding the DIMS system in an AR 15-6 report on possible Camp Delta SOP violations in the wake of the 2006 "suicides." In late August 2006, the Army's AR 15-6 report was completed. Its section on DIMS was as follows:

"The Detainee Information Management System (DIMS) is the primary system for Camp Delta guards to record everything related to detainee and events that occur in the blocks, as well as the primary system employed by the JDG staff in performance of staff duties....

"At the cell block level, guards enter log entries into DIMS at the beginning of each shift, and throughout the shift. These entries are reviewed by Platoon Leaders, Sergeants of the Guard, Block NCOs, and sometimes the FGIW officer, before and during the watch. Because DIMS entries are mandatory, continually updated, and thorough, they provide a significant source of information to the events that occurred on 9 June 2006."

In a June 22, 2006 NCIS Investigative Action report on the detainee deaths earlier that month – a "Review of Standard Operation Procedures for Camp Delta, JTF-GTMO" – the NCIS reporter explained that DIMS was "used to annotate everything related to a Detainee.... Items to be recorded in DIMS are 'Meal refusals, conversations, behavioral problems, leadership, prayer leadership, teaching, preaching, rule breaking, coordination with other detainees, movements, requests, everything.'" The computer database also contained important documents by the guard force (the Joint Detention Group), including a Daily Block NCO checklist, Random Headcount reports, and Significant Activity Sheets."[52]

The NCIS review concluded, "information related to incidents of 10Jun06... should be recorded in the DIMS system."

The by-now hoary computer rule – "garbage in, garbage out" – is worth considering as well when it comes to DIMS entries. So, for instance, and crucially, according to the Army AR 15-6 report on the 2006 "suicides," investigators found that the 2350 (or 11:50pm) random headcount of detainees the night of the 2006 "suicides" had been "falsely reported" by "an unknown member of the Alpha Block guard team." Such headcounts, recorded in DIMS, "required immediate visual confirmation of detainee [two or three words redacted] in each cell."

There were other inconsistencies in the DIMS logs as well. DIMS records showed only two detainees had rags in their mouths at their deaths, while other reports by NCIS say three detainees who died that night in June 2006 had rags.[53]

According to investigators, "no guard remembers performing the 2350 headcount." Reading further, we see that no one could be linked to the 2017 random headcount, either, though the AR 15-6 report notes only the 2350 headcount was false. And yet both of these reports were there in DIMS. This is a crucial finding of falsification of evidence contemporaneous to events in the 2006 detainee deaths. It should have been a red flag. But Army investigators minimized the fact that someone was lying about the headcount of cellblock prisoners, three of whom would soon be found dead. Instead, they found the falsification of the cellblock census (which is what a random headcount is) to be "insignificant." Their reasoning? Medical teams had concluded the bodies were already dead an hour before the 2350 headcount was made. They never asked why the headcount was falsified, or explained how they knew it was, or that there was anything strange in the fact the other headcount earlier that night could not be attributed to any member of the guard staff.[54]

In fact, the falsified headcount is not "insignificant" at all if one concludes the detainees' bodies were brought back dead or nearly dead from another site in Guantanamo, such as the notorious "Camp No," as former Guantanamo guard Joe Hickman maintains in public press accounts and in his own book.

The problems with DIMS that surfaced in the 2006 "suicides" are worth remembering as we turn back to the situation with Al Hanashi.

A NCIS interim report, dated as early as two days after Al Hanashi died, described the shutdown of DIMS at the time of Al Hanashi's death: "The chronology of events surrounding the death of V/Al Hanashi were not logged into the DIMS system allegedly due to an NCIS agent requesting no additional logging take place." ("V/Al Hanashi," a term used throughout NCIS reports, stands for "Victim Al Hanashi.") Without the DIMS records, there is no way to test the timeline or the veracity of the observations of guards or medical personnel.

The order to halt all logging on the Guantanamo computer database apparently came once Al Hanashi was found unresponsive in his cell and before he was pronounced dead. The individual who made the request was "undetermined."

One individual, whose name was redacted in the FOIA release, was asked to provide the name of the person who made the last DIMS entry for Al Hanashi, but this unnamed person told the NCIS investigator "he would have to send the request through his chain of command." The FOIA record does not show that any name was ever obtained or reported back to NCIS.

Despite all the missing information, in the first weeks of the investigation NCIS determined via witness interviews of guard and medical staff, as well as "death scene processing," that the investigation had "failed to identify any suspicious circumstances surrounding V/Al Hanashi's death."

Despite the claims of no mysterious circumstances, the mystery over who turned off DIMS entries was never cleared up, despite what would be months and even years of further investigation.

"A leader among the detainees"

Mohammed Al Hanashi was a 31-year-old Yemeni national who, as a young man, left Yemen to join the Taliban side in the Afghan civil war. DoD claimed he was affiliated with al-Qaeda, a charge Al Hanashi denied.[55] Captured by the Northern Alliance, he was present at the Qala-i-Jangi prisoner uprising at Mazar-e-Sharif in late November 2001, after which he was transferred to U.S. custody. Imprisoned first at Kandahar Detention Facility, he arrived at Guantanamo on February 7, 2002. He never saw an attorney during his seven plus years at the Cuba-based prison.

In a sworn statement to NCIS, the Chief of Behavioral Services for Guantanamo's Joint Task Force – a man who, as described elsewhere, apparently played a crucial role in Al Hanashi's decision to commit suicide – said the Yemeni detainee was "a leader among the detainees on the [BHU] tier. For example, the guard force was working with him to get input on detainee recreation and television schedules. He seemed to enjoy doing this."

Another guard called Al Hanashi a "pseudo-leader" of the detainees at the BHU, and said he helped "facilitate prayer time."

At the same time, according to medical records, Al Hanashi complained about guards "interrupting prayer time by talking to other guard force members or knocking on cell doors."

On the day he died, according to a purported suicide note found at the time of his death, Al Hanashi complained to the Chief of Behavioral Services about imminent changes to administrative rules in the BHU. According to the Chief, "in his mind, the BHU was now the same as the camps."

What did he mean by "now the same as the camps?"

The standard operating procedures for prisoners in the non-hospital portion of Guantanamo included varying levels of prisoner treatment, with privileges and communal living allowed for cooperative prisoners, and harsh treatment (including months of solitary confinement) and removal of privileges and "comfort items" for prisoners deemed non-cooperative. The latter included the many hunger strikers in the prison, of which Al Hanashi had been one.

The inpatient hospital unit of Guantanamo apparently had offered a refuge from harsher treatment, at least temporarily. For Al Hanashi, the threat to turn the hospital over to the mainstream regime inside the prison camp was too much.

Gitmo Psychologist: I "usually" walk away "when a detainee accuses staff of torture"

Al Hanashi had more to say in his suicide note. At the meeting only hours before he died, he told the Behavioral Services Chief, who was a psychologist, that he felt he "was being tortured." The Chief explained in a statement to NCIS investigators, "In this case, to avoid an argument with [redacted, but likely "ISN 78," Al Hanashi's ID at Guantanamo], I walked away from him without a response. This is what I usually do when a detainee accuses staff of torture."

The chief said this "was the last time I saw [Al Hanashi] alive."

According to the previously declassified autopsy report[56] on Al Hanashi's death, he had been on a hunger strike since January 2009. In previous hunger strikes, his weight had fallen as low as 70 pounds, and he was fed via feeding tube at least part of that time.[57]

As we shall see, along with the other detainees considered in this book, Al Amri and Latif, Al Hanashi had some pretty dramatic weight fluctuations during the course of his incarceration. These fluctuations to some degree will correspond with periods of hunger striking, but not all of the fluctuations correlate with that, and it raises the question as to exactly what was happening with either the measurements or the food regimen at Guantanamo.

For instance, Al Hanashi's weight on admission, February 8, 2002, was supposedly 124 pounds. On August 15, 2002, his weight measured 116. But two days later, he supposedly weighed in at 89 pounds, an incredible 27 pound fluctuation in two days! By September 11, 2002, his weight is recorded back up to 112. His weight continued to fluctuate in the hundred and teens through June 2003. But in July 2003, Al Hanashi's weight shot up to 130, an eighteen pounds gain in one month.

Another period of sharp fluctuation occurred in 2005, a year of known increased hunger striking in the camp. In February, he weighed in at 115. In March, he was 141; in April he weighed 140. Then, in May 2005, he was back down to 109.

Sometimes, the dramatic weight fluctuations occurred within a single day. On July 22, 2005, Guantanamo officials measured an all-time low for Al Hanashi of 70 pounds. But the very next day, he supposedly weighed 108 pounds. It is difficult, even with forced feeding, to imagine 38 pounds of fluids could have been pumped into Al Hanashi within a single day. Despite the wild fluctuations, thus far no investigation has looked into what was actually happening inside the medical clinic where prisoners were enterally or forced fed.

* * * *

Al Hanashi entered Guantanamo's detainee behavioral hospital unit on January 10, 2009 for "suicidal ideations," according to a review of his medical records. Over the next approximately five months, he would make three suicide attempts, as noted in the NCIS investigatory record. The autopsy report, however, states there were five attempts.

Military medical examiners concluded Al Hanashi asphyxiated himself by wrapping the elastic waistband of his underwear around his neck.

But the particulars of what happened contemporaneously to the events are unknown, except as recounted to investigators after the fact. Without the DIMS records, there is no way to test the timeline or the veracity of the observations of guards or medical personnel. What we have left are the statements given by guards and medical staff to NCIS investigators about what happened.

At least one guard, identified as Hamby in report materials, told an NCIS agent he saw Hanashi writing a letter the night he died. Hanashi "seemed 'down' because he was a little more quiet than normal. [Hamby] stated that V/Al Hanashi was usually talkative. According to [Hamby] V/Al Hanashi wrote a letter until approximately 2050." This account differs from the autopsy report, which said Al Hanashi "appeared, to the guard, in 'good spirits' and did not appear upset."

Yet another guard, identified only as an African-American member of the Naval Expeditionary Guard Battalion (NEGB), told NCIS that the night of Hanashi's death everything was "normal." Hanashi "was in cell two and he seemed in good spirits." This guard claimed he had seen Hanashi "when he was about to do something disruptive and I did not observe that behavior that night." He wasn't upset; "he was not pacing in his cell, or praying loudly that evening." He "did not see [Hanashi] writing any letters or doing anything out of his normal pattern."

Another guard, identified as Herrera, told NCIS investigators "that V/Al Hanashi complained about the BHU on a regualr [sic] basis and seemed very 'frustrated' with the administrative process at JTF-GTMO. [Herrera] advised that V/Al Hanashi had no problems or specific issues with the NEGB or any particualr [sic] guard at the BHU." Herrera also said Hanashi had "no apparent ill feelings towards" the guards. He "was not aware of any guard having issues with or harboring ill feelings towards V/Al Hanashi."

Yet another guard, also unnamed, told investigators, "I did not notice anything in particular about [Al Hanashi's] demeanor or conduct to indicate that he was considering suicide. He seemed to be acting normal." But the prisoner did ask to see a nurse, with whom he was friendly, and this guard got the nurse as asked, and later observed her give Hanashi a pill (reportedly an Ambien). The guard watched Al Hanashi take the pill, according to standard operating procedures.

"Mentally tortured"

According to a statement to NCIS investigators given by this same nurse, whose name was redacted from records, she "forewarned" the Chief of Behavioral Health Services, and the BHU guards about Al Hanashi's suicidal thoughts. "H. did try to commit suicide on 2-3 other occasions," she stated. "He had tried to hang himself, and he had 'slammed his head against a fence bolt while in the BHU recreation area.'"

In an early NCIS report from January 2010 – written before all the DIMS records for the day of Al Hanashi's death and the day after went missing – an investigating agent noted in a report that the final entry from the DIMS record on the evening Al Hanashi died was "Received medication." The time was 2118, or 9:18 at night. After that, the DIMS record went silent.

The nurse explained in her statement to NCIS that Al Hanashi had told her the night he died that he was upset she had told camp officials about his wish to meet with her privately at noon on June 10. The request, made approximately two weeks earlier, seemed strange to the nurse, until she found upon consultation that June 10, 2006 was the anniversary date when three detainees were found dead in their cells – suicide victims, DoD maintained.

The nurse told the distraught Hanashi "she was required as a part of her job to provide all information about possible patient safety issues to the BHU staff." The nurse told NCIS that Hanashi "seemed fine after her explanation."

But she also reported that he didn't want to talk further after that conversation. While she also said it wasn't unusual "for V/Al Hanashi to not want to talk.... V/Al Hanashi assured her he was not mad and apologized to her for not wanting to talk." Instead, he just wanted to sleep. But, if it is was normal for him to not want to talk, why did he apologize for it? Why did he have to reassure her he was not upset?

Approximately 45 minutes later, around 10:00 pm, or 2200 military time, one of the guards called out for help when he saw Hanashi lying motionless in his cell. Other guards and medical personnel were called and attempts made to revive him, to no avail. A narrow piece of cloth wrapped around his neck was cut off.

Al Hanashi must have looked grisly. His lips were blue, his neck swollen. There was a trickle of blood coming from his mouth. Guards cut the ligature from around his neck. A psychiatric nurse who arrived on the scene said he saw some "red/purple bruises on the front of V/Al Hanashi's neck."

One corpsman at the scene said he had felt Hanashi still had a weak pulse in his ankles when he arrived. The nurse who last saw Hanashi in his cell that night told NCIS that she "received some conflicting medical information in reference to V/Al Hanashi's vital signs. [Redacted] stated that she initially heard one of the medical personnel say V/Al Hanashi was breathing but she later heard that he was not breathing."

The nurse said she saw no evidence of foul play, nor did she see anyone enter Hanashi's cell before he died. She noted in addition that she saw no evidence of physical abuse or torture of the young Yemeni prisoner, but admitted he "felt he was being mentally tortured by the camp rules and the guards' enforcement of those rules."

One of the guards, a Caucasian assigned to NEGB, who discovered Al Hanashi's body, said he noticed the prone prisoner was "wearing a tan shirt." This was peculiar because he "was not authorized to wear a tee-shirt so the white fabric around his neck caught my attention."

Al Hanashi likely was not supposed to be wearing a t-shirt because only a month earlier he had tried to hang himself using his t-shirt while out in the camp's recreation yard.

According to one guard's testimony, "Due to his suicide attempts, [Al Hanashi] was under constant monitoring by a guard and he was placed in a green self harm suit." But despite warnings by a nurse, and a history of multiple suicide attempts in previous weeks, Al Hanashi was not apparently placed in clothing used on suicidal patients, at least on the day he died.

Attempts to revive Al Hanashi via CPR produced a lot of vomiting and blood. The Senior Medical Officer ordered the patient taken from the Behavioral Health Unit to the Detainee Hospital, where further attempts to revive him failed. The records state that a Dr. Enterprise "called the code" on Al Hanashi at 10:54 pm. One witness said some of those present cried when the final moment came.

According to NCIS investigation notes, "an unknown NCIS" special agent "instructed JTF GTMO personnel... to cease making entries into the DIMS subsequent to the death of V/Al Hanashi. No JTF GTMO personnel were identified as making the claim." A Resident Agent from NCIS who was first on the scene after Al Hanashi was discovered was not identified in any report.

NCIS investigation reports stated, "None of the aforementioned NCIS Special Agents that processed the death scene and/or initiated investigative actions pertaining to captioned investigation claimed that they instructed any JTF GTMO personnel to cease making entries into DIMS of V/Al Hanashi on 01/02 JUN09. In addition, all the aforementioned NCIS Special Agents advised that they would not have given such an instruction."

And yet someone gave the instruction.

"I knew that the only solution is death"

Turning off DIMS entries was a serious violation of Guantanamo procedures. The 2004 Camp Delta Standard Operating Procedures manual, released by Wikileaks, has detailed instructions for what should be recorded on DIMS.[58]

Guantanamo authorities watched over detainee behavior very closely. Literally anything of interest was supposed to be recorded in DIMS. The SOP states, "There is always significant activity occurring on a block. There should be no DIMS SIGACT [significant activities] sheet filled out with 'Nothing to report.'"

Despite the finding of missing DIMS material, a small portion of the DIMS logs for the day Al Hanashi died was actually documented in an "Investigative Action" report entitled "Results of Detainee Information Management System Database Review." The report was written two days after Al Hanashi died.

The report described a DIMS log entry for June 1, 2009 (now "lost"), made approximately three hours before he died, which showed Al Hanashi was briefed "regarding enforcement of BHU regulations that were to start" the very next day. The new rules would be very upsetting to Al Hanashi.

Al Hanashi mentioned the change in rules inside the mental health hospital unit for detainees in a purported suicide note found at the scene. He also complained about them to a nurse approximately an hour or two before he died, as described above.

As with other irregularities in the NCIS investigation, Al Hanashi's suicide note was "found" in different places. In one account, the note was found on the floor of the cell. Another account said it was found in a blue folder in an administrative section of the Behavioral Health Unit. Yet another account said the note was found "within the medical waste just outside the cell door." (The idea that evidence would be thrown out in medical waste is a theme we will encounter again when we look at the death of Abdul Rahman al Amri.)

In this "suicide note," written "In the name of Allah the merciful the compassionate!", Al Hanashi wrote that he went into the Guantanamo psychiatric hospital unit "because I could not support the rules of the camps." He may be referring to the harsh "Behavioral Management" rules[59] that gave or withdrew from prisoners their personal items, including toilet paper, and privileges based on their cooperation with camp authorities.

According to the Camp Delta SOP, "The Detainee Classification System is a five level system of rewards based on the premise that a detainee's behavior determines the privileges they are allowed. As the detainee adapts to the rules of the camp, his conduct will earn him more privileges."

Privileges allowed or withdrawn based on behavioral criteria included exercise and recreation, hot meals, linens, extra toilet paper, shampoo, and placement in solitary confinement, or Secure Housing Unit (SHU). A "Behavioral Management Plan" for each detainee was implemented as soon as a new prisoner arrived.

The purpose of this plan, according to camp authorities in the SOP manual, was "to enhance and exploit the disorientation and disorganization felt by a newly arrived detainee in the interrogation process." Even after the first phase of the plan had expired, a behavioral plan remained in place to "continue the process of isolating the detainee and fostering dependence on the interrogator."

Putting camp psychiatric hospital patients under general camp rules was a significant change at that time from previous policy. For instance, the 2004 rules state, "Any proposed discipline for detainees under the care of the Detention Hospital Psychologist requires consultation between the senior on-duty psychology staff member and the on-duty CO prior to imposing discipline. Detainees being treated as mental health patients will only have Basic Issue Items, authorized CIs, and/or Authorized Activities taken away as a medical necessity…"

In his note, Al Hanashi admitted he had "tried to kill myself in camp 6 and in camp 5," stating he and the other patients in the psychiatric unit "are sick." He said he had heard that prison personnel "made mockery of prayer," but he didn't hear it personally because he "was out walking."

Amnesty International has described Camp 5 as "an isolation and interrogation facility for 'non-compliant' detainees that opened in October 2004." Prisoners in Camp 5 were confined in isolation nearly 24 hours per day in "small, enclosed cells" with "solid metal doors" and "a small window looking onto an interior corridor." There was also a "narrow frosted window on the outside wall" which provided some natural light, though no actual view."[60]

Camp 6 was opened in December 2006, and conditions there were even harsher. Also aimed at near total isolation, the cells were noisy, with steel floors and walls. There were no windows, only a strip of glass that looked out onto the corridor and the patrol of guards. With no natural light, and constant florescent lighting in the cells, a prisoner couldn't know what time of day it was. A Chinese Muslim prisoner at Guantanamo called Camp 6 "a dungeon above the ground."[61]

(Just as this book was going to press, a Pentagon spokesman said that as of August 19, 2016, the maximum-security wing of Camp 5 had been closed, and the prisoners transferred to Camp 6. As of September 11, 2016, a total of 46 detainees remain in Camp 6, while 15 former CIA "high-value" prisoners remain in Guantanamo's secretive Camp 7. Camp 5 is undergoing multi-million dollar renovations as a medical facility.)[62]

Al Hanashi then addressed the issue of the rules changes, changes that apparently led him to consider suicide. In addition, he gave his version of the account of his encounter with the Chief of Behavioral Services the day he killed himself, recounted above. In Al Hanashi's version, the decision of the head of Behavioral Services to walk away led to a fateful conclusion:

"I have heard from the guards that are going to apply the same rules on us as the other camps but when the highest ranking officer in the camp came and talked to me while I was walking he informed me that this camp will have the same rules as the others, and when I asked the help of the psychologist who was present, he said the rules will apply on everybody then he left without saying anything more. Even the officer who was close to him was surprised by his inappropriate behavior as someone who is supposed to be in a humanitarian position. At that time I knew that the only solution is death before they transgress on our religion the way they do in the other camps. I had wanted to write a lot more but I feel depressed[.]"

"Investigative Action"

Within a few days after Al Hanashi's death, NCIS investigators began their own investigation into why Guantanamo personnel, presumably both guards and medical personnel in the psychiatric unit, were told to stop entering information on the circumstances surrounding the detainee's death.

According to a June 3, 2009 "Investigative Action" report, "Results of Detainee Information Management System Database Review," an unidentified agent wrote, "The chronology of events surrounding the death of V/Al Hanashi were not logged into the DIMS system allegedly due to an NCIS agent requesting no additional logging take place. It is undetermined who actually requested no logging take place during the investigative stage. Participating agents [redacted] and [redacted] deny making such a request; however, Resident Agent in charge [redacted] was the first Special Agent on the scene." (All redactions were made by NCIS in their FOIA release.)

By November 2, 2009, Al Hanashi's case had progressed to initial review by a "Death Review Panel" convened at NCIS's Southeast Field Office in Mayport, Florida. The panel determined "additional investigative leads should be conducted." Besides further documentation from the autopsy and the death scene, the panel tasked investigators to "contact NCIS Special Agent [redacted] and clarify her actions during her initial response to V/Al Hanashi's death and the utilization of the detainee's Information Management System Database (DIMS)."

On January 8, 2010, another "Investigative Action" reports on two telephonic interviews with a female NCIS agent at the scene of Al Hanashi's death, presumably the same Special Agent mentioned by the Death Review Panel.

This agent told the investigating NCIS agent "she did not instruct any JTF GTMO personnel to cease making entries into the DIMS pertaining to V/Al Hanashi." Furthermore, investigators wrote, "she would not have issued such an order even if she had the authority to do so citing her efforts to encourage documentation."

This same agent added she didn't know of any other NCIS agent who would have given such an order.

Interestingly, there were members of other agencies present at the time. According to the female NCIS agent, when she arrived at the death scene along with another NCIS agent, there were two agents of the Army Criminal Investigation Command (CID), and a FBI Special Agent "already present at the BHU."

The female agent making the telephonic statement added she "doubted that any of the aforementioned personnel would have issues [sic] such a directive."

Who Made the Last DIMS Entry?

In a follow-up to the aforementioned interviews, on January 13, 2010, another "Investigative Action," reporting on the results of an interview with an unnamed NCIS officer, stated that the RA (presumably the NCIS Resident Agent at Guantanamo) "requested" yet another unnamed individual to find out who had made the last DIMS entry on Al Hanashi, and see if that person received the order to forego DIMS entries, and if so, from whom.

According to the January 13 report, "[Redacted] advised that he would have to send the request through his chain of command. [Redacted] was instructed to contact RA if he had difficulty obtaining the requested information."

There is no record of this request up the chain of command ever being further discussed or acted upon.

According to a February 17, 2005 article by American Forces Press Service, published by the Department of Defense, "DIMS is managed from Camp Delta's Detention Operations Center.... the system allows guards and officers to view information on a variety of categories broken down by camp, cellblock, cell or detainee."[63]

The information includes whether "medical personnel or other visitors have been on the block or are scheduled to be on the block," and includes information on each detainee's "country of origin, the types of comfort items he's allowed, and medical and behavioral notes."

The 2004 version of the Standard Operating Procedures (SOP) manual for Guantanamo,[64] released by Wikileaks in 2007, describes procedures for use of DIMS.

The manual notes, "How the detainee reacted, observation by other detainees, and other potentially relevant observations will be annotated in DIMS."

"Relevant observations" of detainee behavior to be recorded include requests for copies of the Koran; refusals to let their cell be searched; refusal of a meal; visits by non-block personnel; and anything deemed a "significant activity."

A list of "significant activities" include banging on the cell, "showing reverence to another detainee," displays of "extreme emotion," requesting an interpreter, and harming oneself, among others. The SOP notes, "All data entries via DIMS must be specific and complete."

The information logged into DIMS can be quite specific and involves almost any action by a detainee. For instance, the manual states any "request for the librarian, interpreter, or Chaplain… will be logged in DIMS." The SOP makes special mention of recording of books issued, including the Koran.

How a detainee reacts, observations from other detainees, and any "other potentially relevant observations will be annotated appropriately in the DIMS significant activities menu."

DIMS entries can be very specific and detailed. For instance, the manual describes procedures for the shackling of prisoners: "If a detainee is required to kneel, the Block NCO will note in DIMS whenever a detainee is required to kneel to be shackled. The notation will include the time, ISN, type of escort (shower & exercise, reservation, etc.) and a BRIEF reason as to the deviation from shackling in the standing position."

While NCIS now states that the DIMS logs on Al Hanashi are missing, as noted above an investigative report two days after Al Hanashi died shows that a review of DIMS records by an NCIS Reporting Agent for the day Al Hanashi died did in fact occur. This report found "No significant events involving" Al Hanashi, "including physical altercations with JTF GTMO personnel."

Below are reproduced the last DIMS entries for Al Hanashi's final hours, as reported by the NCIS agent (hours are in military time):

"01JUN09/1833 - Received brief regarding enforcement of BHU regulations starting on 02JUN09

"01JUN09/1920 - Escorted from Rec Yard back to cell

"01JUN09/2100 - Ate evening meal

"01JUN09/2118 - Received medication"

Medications mentioned in the NCIS documents include psychiatric drugs for sleep and anxiety, including Ambien, Klonopin, Benadryl, Haldol, Ativan, and Xanax. According to Hanashi's autopsy, [65] the tranquilizers Klonopin and Ativan were present in his blood at the time of his death, though not in amounts considered to be excessive.

Questions About Physical Evidence

Approximately two weeks after Al Hanashi died, investigators sent evidence from the investigation via U.S. registered mail to the Army Criminal Investigation Laboratory in Forest Park, Georgia. The package generated a memorandum to the Special Agent in Charge at NCIS, Guantanamo, citing "improper packaging" of the evidence.

The evidence included the ligature, fashioned from the underwear Al Hanashi purportedly used to strangle himself to death, as well as written materials by the deceased, including his "last will" and suicide note.

According to the Army lab, NCIS had failed to package their examination request properly. But worse, the cardboard box that contained the evidence "was not sealed properly." The memo stated, "Pieces of cellophane tape used to secure three sides allowed access to the inside of the shipping container."

The lab reminded NCIS that "all open edges" must be sealed, and "there must be identifying markings over the seals to detect unauthorized intrusion." Using cellophane tape is not allowed.

Despite the irregularities, the evidence was examined and apparently accepted as determinative in the investigation of Al Hanashi's death, which was attributed to self-strangulation.

Never explained was why Al Hanashi even had access to normal cotton brief underwear, since according to an October 17, 2007 article by Carol Rosenberg at the Miami Herald,[66] after the three detainees were discovered dead in 2006, officially from "suicide," Guantanamo officials changed "captives' underwear from more elastic briefs to cotton boxers less liable to be used in a hanging."

A Reuters report[67] from the same period stated that after the 2006 deaths "the prisoners' underwear was switched from briefs with wide elastic bands to boxers made of flimsier fabric that rips under stress." Pictures released by NCIS from the Al Hanashi investigation represent the underwear as typical cotton elastic briefs, not boxer shorts. The pictures taken by NCIS investigators show the briefs have an elastic band.

The sudden reporting on detainee underwear in fall 2007 was due to one of those bizarre news stories that Guantanamo has spawned over the years. At the time, the press had a field day with the seemingly humorous story.

According to reports that surfaced in September of that year, two detainee attorneys, Clive Stafford Smith and Zachary Katznelson of the British human rights group Reprieve, were accused by Guantanamo authorities of having smuggled contraband underwear to two of their clients.

The underwear, a reportedly stretchy type made by the company Under Armour, and a Speedo, which came with a tie string, were decidedly not the kind of underwear allowed in the prison. Smith and Katznelson denied they had anything to do with the appearance of the contraband undergarments, with Smith quipping that his job involved "legal briefs, not the other sort."[68] Meanwhile, DoD officials played up the potential harm in the use of such materials as could be found in regular men's underwear or briefs.

Navy Capt. Patrick McCarthy, Staff Judge Advocate during the 2006 and 2007 "suicides," who told the press he had personally seen all four of the detainee "suicides" hanging in their cells, was adamant about the underwear danger.

"There was a Speedo in the camp and someone can hang himself with it," McCarthy told the press. "The Speedo also has a drawstring on it. The drawstring can be used to tie the Speedo, the noose apparatus up onto a vent."[69]

The NCIS report entitled "Results of Review of Evidence and Command Materials," dated June 4, 2009,[70] stated that NCIS was given an unaltered sample of the kind of underwear purportedly worn by Al Hanashi. "An unidentified command member" provided the sample briefs during the course of the autopsy. The underwear was a "men's white-colored brief underwear," manufactured by the Bob Barker Company, Inc. in North Carolina. The Barker briefs were "constructed similarly to common men's brief underwear," including an elastic waistband with "two dark-colored parallel lines on the top edge of the band."

Guantanamo officials offered the Barker underwear as an example of the same kind of underwear that Al Hanashi allegedly used to strangle himself, using the elastic band as a ligature. The autopsy doctors concluded the ligature was indeed the same kind of material as the proffered brief's elastic band, and NCIS concurred.

No one ever mentioned that the underwear in question was not the appropriate kind of underwear used by detainees at that time. Such disinterest is highly inconsistent with the Pentagon panic induced over the report of Speedos and other improper underwear used by some Guantanamo detainees, and concern over how such underwear could be used for purposes of self-harm.

Whatever the origin of the 2007 contraband underwear, the military's investigation into the incident was either inconclusive or its findings suppressed. But one can't wonder if there were any connections with the man who less than two years later would be said to strangle himself to death with the elastic band of his underwear.

In reports filed throughout the Al Hanashi investigation, NCIS stated that Guantanamo command officers were kept informed of unfolding events. It is not known if that included issues with the handling of evidence, or problems with the DIMS entries, nor do we know if senior command officials were themselves interviewed.

Some of the answers to the questions raised in this book might surface in the Army's own AR 15-6 investigation into Al Hanashi's death. A FOIA request for that material was filed in January 2013, but processing of the request with U.S. Southern Command is still ongoing.

Chapter 3
Al Hanashi's "testament" and suicide note

As transcribed from NCIS documents

The night of 04/01/2009   In the name of Allah the merciful the compassionate!

Praise to Allah lord of all creation and peace and prayers upon the noblest of all messengers and prophets!

To my kind family, my father, my mother, my brothers and sisters and all my relatives, First of all I urge you to be devoted to Allah almighty, I urge you to be prompt with your prayers and to always pray in group, I urge you with charity because it extinguishes Allah' wrath as water extinguishes fire, I urge for compassion for the orphans the poor and the needy. Beware of the malicious gossip because it is the biggest sin and it is the cause of dividing people, its consequences are great at the Day of Judgment. I also urge with good moral values, politeness and heed and respecting those who are older than you and show compassion for those who are younger. Raise your children well in all aspects, intellectually and physically in order for them to live in society with a sound mind and a healthy body that can resist any illnesses.

I urge you to look out for the neighbor even if he is a Jew. I have urged your blessed messenger. Respect his rights regardless of any of his short comings toward you. Do not eat while he is hungry and do not wear clothes while he is naked. That is our duty toward him. The messenger of Allah, peace and Allah's prayers upon him "angel Gabriel was urging me so much to care for the neighbor I thought he (Gabriel) was going to make him (the neighbor) inheritor"

As for me I don't remember I owe a debt to anyone except [approximately 3 or 4 words censored] I think I owe her something but I know she had forgiven me but just in case someone tells you I owe them a debt I want you to pay him.

I had wanted to write a letter for each one of you but I was afraid to forget anyone person and he would think I have something against him. My regards to everyone! My father had said "my regards had grown from the hardness of rocks" but me; I say my regards had grown from the hardness of prison.

Do not be sad for my death O family! Allah almighty said "every soul will taste death".

Life is no good without honor and a poet put it:

"I have sworn either to live with honor and dignity or you may taste my bones."

Anyway O family, I am well aware of my situation and of my circumstances. I have not come to this without having been convinced by legal scholars.

One has no blessing in life if one is deprived from certain joys.

O family, beware of arrogance and be modest! One poet said:

The fruitful wheat leans modestly   and the heads of the empty ones rise high

Finally, I would love to advice and talk to you more but you are more aware of everything. This however is a legal bequest that had to be done.

My best regards to my father and to my mother!

Your son

[Undated, but believed to be the day of his death, June 1, 2009]

In the name of Allah the merciful the compassionate!

I have not come from camp 5 except because I could not support the rules of the camps

I have tried to kill myself in camp 6 and in camp 5. Anyway, all my brothers came from the camps for the same reason; as such we mean that we are sick

I have heard that in camp 5 they made mockery of prayer but I was out walking. I have heard from the guards that are going to apply the same rules on us as the other camps but when the highest ranking officer in the camp came and talked to me while I was walking he informed me that this camp will have the same rules as the others, and when I asked the help of the psychologist who was present, he said the rules will apply on everybody then he left without saying anything more. Even the officer who was close to him was surprised by his inappropriate behavior as someone who is supposed to be in a humanitarian position. At that time I knew that the only solution is death before they transgress on our religion the way they do in the other camps. I had wanted to write a lot more but I feel depressed

My testament is in the bleu folder.[71]

Chapter 4
"The only solution is death": Al Hanashi's Final Days

On April 1, 2009, 31-year-old Mohammed Al Hanashi sat in his hospital cell at Guantanamo writing what reads like his last will and testament. The tiny room is nearly all white. There is a sink, a toilet, and a steel door with a slot for food and medications. A light shone at all times, day and night.

Probably unknown to Al Hanashi, in a grotesque coincidence, a USO tour of Guantanamo with both the 2008 winners of the Miss USA and Miss Universe contests had just visited the camp. Dayana Mendoza, the Miss Universe winner from Venezuela, caused some controversy with a blog piece about her visit.

"We visited the Detainees camps and we saw the jails, where they shower, how the [sic] recreate themselves with movies, classes of art, books. It was very interesting," Ms. Mendoza wrote.

"The water in Guantánamo Bay is soooo beautiful! It was unbelievable; we were able to enjoy it for at least an hour. We went to the glass beach, and realized the name of it comes from the little pieces of broken glass from hundred of years ago. It is pretty to see all the colors shining with the sun....

"I didn't want to leave, it was such a relaxing place, so calm and beautiful."[72]

How impossibly distant was the experience of detainee number 078.

"In the name of Allah the merciful the compassionate!" Al Hanashi wrote in Arabic. He had been imprisoned at that point for over seven years. Some may think, well, there are literally thousands of prisoners in U.S. prisons who have been imprisoned as long and longer, who have spent years in isolation. Such prisoners often have been seriously damaged by their experience,[73] but the Guantanamo experience took matters even farther.

The detainee had not been charged with any crime. He had not met with any attorney. The length of his imprisonment remained unknown and indeterminate. He was thousands of miles from home, held by a foreign power, manipulated in a regime that fancied itself a "battle lab" in the war on terror.

The detainee, Yemeni prisoner Mohammad Ahmed Abdullah Saleh Al Hanashi, was one of hundreds still imprisoned at the U.S. Department of Defense "strategic interrogation" prison site at Guantanamo.

He'd been on hunger strike and fed via tube for some time (we don't know if he was forcibly fed or not, but another detainee has written that he was[74]). Now he pondered his death, most likely via suicide. Or perhaps he thought he would die from the hunger strike, or as a victim of torture.

Al Hanashi pondered the "hardness" of life at Guantanamo. "Do not be sad for my death O family!" he wrote. "Allah almighty said 'every soul will taste death.'"

"Life is no good without honor and a poet put it: 'I have sworn either to live with honor and dignity or you may taste my bones.'"

From the document, it appears Al Hanashi had considered suicide deeply, and the deprivation of prison life at Guantanamo proved too much for him. "Anyway O family, I am well aware of my situation and of my circumstances," he wrote. "I have not come to this without having been convinced by legal scholars.

"One has no blessing in life if one is deprived from certain joys."

According to his 2008 JTF-GTMO detainee assessment (one of hundreds released by Wikileaks),[75] Al Hanashi was born in February 1978. He grew up in Yemen and graduated secondary school in 1995 or 1996. "After graduation… [he] worked for his father on the family farm where they raised livestock and grew watermelons, tomatoes, corn and other crops," though the detainee assessment said he told a Yemeni delegation to Guantanamo that he used to be in the military.

In general, intelligence officials at Guantanamo thought Al Hanashi minimized his role fighting in forces associated with Al Qaeda. As a result, they judged him as "High risk," a threat to the U.S. and its interests and allies, as well as "A High threat from a detention perspective." (They would state the same thing about Al Amri.)

According to Guantanamo expert Andy Worthington, Al Hanashi "was one of around 50 prisoners at Guantanamo who had survived a massacre at Qala-i-Janghi, a fort in northern Afghanistan, at the end of November 2001, when, after the surrender of the city of Kunduz, several hundred foreign fighters surrendered to General Rashid Dostum, one of the leaders of the Northern Alliance, in the mistaken belief that they would be allowed to return home. Instead, they were imprisoned in Qala-i-Janghi, a nineteenth century mud fort in Mazar-e-Sharif, and when some of the men started an uprising against their captors, which led to the death of a CIA operative, U.S. Special Forces, working with the Northern Alliance and British Special Forces, called in bombing raids to suppress the uprising, leading to hundreds of deaths. The survivors — who, for the most part, had not taken part in the fighting — took shelter in the basement of the fort, where they endured further bombing, and they emerged only after many more had died when the basement was set on fire and then flooded."[76]

This was the same prison revolt and subsequent massacre by U.S., British and Northern Alliance forces where the so-called "American Taliban," John Walker Lind, was also captured and later tortured by U.S. operatives.[77]

According to his Combatant Status Review Tribunal (CSRT) record,[78] Al Hanashi went to Afghanistan to fight for the Taliban in early 2001. He was 23 years old.

Al Hanashi told Guantanamo officials he never heard about Al Qaeda until he read media reports while on the front lines in Afghanistan. He explained that he fought against the Northern Alliance, but said he never killed anybody. After surviving Qala-i-Janghi, he was shipped off to Shabraghan Prison, where he spent the next four weeks or so recuperating in the prison hospital. Also in the hospital with Al Hanashi were victims of a transfer of Northern Alliance prisoners from Kunduz, the survivors of a purported war crime by Dostum's forces (possibly with the knowledge or connivance of U.S. Special Forces), as thousands of prisoners were "stuffed into closed metal shipping containers and given no food or water; many suffocated while being trucked to the prison. Other prisoners were killed when guards shot into the containers," according to a New York Times story.[79]

Did al Hanashi talk with survivors of the Dostum mass killings? Did he hear tales of U.S. Special Operations soldiers or officers involved? According to his JTF-GTMO detainee assessment, an area of "possible exploitation" in his ongoing incarceration was the "Uprising at Mazar-e-Sharif and detainee's reported leadership" there. The claims about "leadership" came from the interrogation of John Walker Lindh, who supposedly told interrogators that Al Hanashi had helped negotiate the surrender of prisoners at Qala-i-Janghi.

Appended to a section of the assessment obtained by Wikileaks is an "Analyst Note," which stated, "If detainee was truly in a situation to negotiate for others, he may have been in a more significant leadership position than reported."

The question of the level of leadership Al Hanashi exerted was brought up both by outside observers (like the former detainee Binyam Mohamed) and, as noted in the released NCIS interviews, by Guantanamo guard and medical personnel. In addition, as we have seen, when Guantanamo officials decided to change the policies for psychiatrically hospitalized detainees, bringing them into alignment with rules for the rest of the camp, a top Guantanamo official came to the Behavioral Health Unit to discuss the situation with Al Hanashi.

Some of the statements made about Al Hanashi can be taken with a grain of salt. Former Guantanamo inmate, Binyam Mohamed, who knew him, has said he didn't believe the 31-year-old Yemeni force-fed hunger striker committed suicide. He told the journalist Naomi Wolf recently that reports that Al Hanashi was "an upbeat person with no mental problems and would never have considered suicide."[80] The documentary record from Guantanamo doesn't support that conclusion.

According to a July 30, 2009 news report, "Mohamed refuses to believe that Saleh committed suicide and the U.S. military refuses to say how he allegedly took his life. 'He was patient and encouraged others to be the same,' Binyam said."[81]

Mohamed also had a different tale about how Al Hanashi came to be in the Behavioral Health Unit. He told reporters, "I was asked if I wanted to represent the prisoners on camp issues such as hunger strikes and other contentious issues. I declined, as did most. But poor Wadhah [Al Hanashi] agreed, wanting to help his brothers the best he could. Little did he realize that if they didn't get their way he would be the one sacrificed."

Regardless of how accurate Binyam Mohamed's narrative of events was, he certainly understood the prison's environmental pressures, and he has held the U.S. military accountable for Al Hanashi's death, as suicide was so improbable under the conditions of detainee confinement. Mohamed pointed out that "Everything that someone could use to hurt himself has been removed from the cell, and a guard watches each prisoner 24 hours a day, in person and on videotape. In light of this, I am amazed that the U.S. government has the audacity to describe Wadhah's death categorically as an 'apparent suicide.'"

Another odd coincidence surrounding Al Hanashi's death concerns the transfer of Ahmed Khalfan Ghailani, a "high-value" detainee, who has been at Guantanamo since September 2006, to a New York federal court, only a week after Al Hanashi was found not breathing in Guantanamo's psych ward. Ghailani was facing charges concerning his alleged role in the 1998 bombings of U.S. embassies in Tanzania and Kenya.

The link between Ghailani and Al Hanashi is significant for at least one reason: According to Andy Worthington, Ghailani, who was tortured in the CIA's black site prisons, fingered Al Hanashi in 2005 as having been at "the al-Farouq camp [the main training camp for Arabs, associated in the years before 9/11 with Osama bin Laden] in 1998-99 prior to moving on to the front lines in Kabul."

But according to Al Hanashi and all other sources, Al Hanashi came to Afghanistan only in early 2001. Hence, his possible testimony at a trial in New York City, establishing that Ghailani's admissions were false, and likely coerced by torture, may have been a hindrance to a government bent on convicting the supposed bomber. Interestingly, as Worthington points out, the other four embassy bombers were not kept in CIA black prisons or tortured, but convicted in a U.S. court for the bombings in May 2001.

(Ghailani himself was acquitted of all but one of 280 counts in the embassy bombings, as the courts refused to admit a witness whose identification came via torture of Ghailani while he was held prisoner in a secret CIA prison. Even so, he was sentenced to life in prison for one count of conspiracy to destroy government buildings and property. Today, he is imprisoned at the ADX Supermax prison in Florence, Colorado.)

Al Hanashi's death, coming only weeks before he was, after seven long years imprisonment, to meet finally with an attorney, brings to mind the untimely death of Ibn al-Sheikh al-Libi, also at first reported as a suicide, in a prison cell in Libya in May 2009, only weeks before Al Hanashi died. Al-Libi, too, was supposed to meet soon with people from the outside, according to a report from Newsweek.[82]

Al-Libi was infamously the source of tortured information that Iraq's Saddam Hussein was gathering weapons of mass destruction, information that Al-Libi later recanted. According to Human Rights Watch, some of their workers met Al-Libi in his prison cell on April 27, 2009, "during a research mission to Libya." Al-Libi "refused to be interviewed, and would say nothing more than: 'Where were you when I was being tortured in American jails"?[83]

As is the case with Al-Libi, the Al Hanashi death has a strange feel to it.

* * * *

On June 1, 2009, three months after writing out his "last testament," Al Hanashi was found seemingly lifeless in his cell. He was taken to the prison hospital, where he was pronounced dead less than an hour later by Dr. Enterprise, a prison physician. (Could that be his actual name? Medical officers routinely used pseudonyms at Guantanamo.) Military authorities said Al Hanashi had committed suicide by self-strangulation.

According to NCIS documents, Al Hanashi told the Chief of Guantanamo's Behavioral Health Unit (BHU) that he felt he was being tortured. They argued about it even on the last day of the detainee's life.

Later that day, only a little over 2 months after writing what NCIS investigators labeled Al Hanashi's "last will and testament,"[84] Al Hanashi wrote what appeared to be a suicide note, but he was too depressed and disheartened to even finish it. Reportedly in silence and quickly, he strangled himself to death with a piece of elastic supposedly taken from his underwear.

In the narrative built by NCIS, Al Hanashi appears haunted by the deaths of three prisoners, supposedly by suicide, on June 10, 2006. While there is evidence that the government's story about those suicides has real holes – as already noted, former Guantanamo guard, Joe Hickman, wrote a book exposing the suppression of and tampering with evidence by the investigating agency – Al Hanashi told medical personnel in the Behavioral Health Unit at Guantanamo that he was supposed to die with the other three detainees on that day, too.

According to a statement given by the Senior Medical Officer, JTF GTMO, she had heard "at various JTF meetings" that Al Hanashi "was on a directed suicide list authored by [redacted]." But Al Hanashi was described as seeking refuge in the detainee mental hospital as a way to escape other detainees "who might have been pressuring him to commit suicide."

No evidence of such a suicide list, or of pressures by other detainees on Al Hanashi to kill himself was included in the FOIA release I received in May 2015 on NCIS investigation into his death. However, in a November 2016 FOIA release of a "Force Protection" document related to Latif's death, a human intelligence "collector's" comment claimed Adnan Latif "was tasked to commit suicide with" Mohammad Al Hanashi in June 2009. No evidence of such a tasking has ever been released or otherwise noted. (See the relevant document, like all the relevant documents mentioned in this book, at GuantanamoTruth.com.)

Back in 2006, camp authorities characterized the three deaths in June as a joint suicide. We see further that camp staff were told that Al Hanashi was on a "directed suicide list." Later, in 2009, camp officials discussed a supposed suicide pact between Al Hanashi and Latif, even on the eve of Latif's own death. Hence, we see a pattern wherein Guantanamo officials discussed links between the various suicides. No evidence of any pact among any of the detainees, or any "directed suicide list," as ever been made public. From internal evidence, the paucity of references to such a pact and the strange, if not suspicious, conditions of the deaths themselves, including efforts to falsify or suppress evidence, it seems very unlikely there ever was any suicide pact between these detainees. The reasons for perpetuating the fiction of such conspiracies within Guantanamo are unknown.

* * * *

I made the original FOIA request upon which this book is based in January 2012. But little did I know at the time, which was two-and-a-half years after Al Hanashi died, that as I filed my FOIA request the NCIS investigation was still underway. Nor did I have any idea the investigation ultimately would take three years to complete. Reading the documents that were finally released, it did not seem NCIS personnel felt much urgency about closing the case. At times, months went by and no investigative activity took place.

When the investigation was finally closed on June 13, 2012, NCIS had to admit in documented form that key portions of the evidence bearing on the chronology of events surrounding Al Hanashi's death had gone missing. As already described, someone – allegedly an investigator from NCIS itself – told Guantanamo personnel to stop entering information on Al Hanashi into a computer database, once his body was discovered. Subsequently, and we don't know exactly when, the logs for the database the day Al Hanashi died, i.e., even before the order to turn off DIMS, and for the entire following day, disappeared entirely. Requests by this author to NCIS to discuss what happened to the missing documents were never answered.

What happened during Al Hanashi's final weeks? How did the detainee who had made numerous suicide attempts in the previous months leading up to his death, finally come to take his life? Did he, in fact, kill himself?

It is worth taking an in-depth, closer look at his death, including actions taken in the days leading up to his death by doctors, nurses and guards. But this remains a provisional narrative, as the complete story is still pointedly unknown, blocked on one hand by government censorship and the failure to release all documentation. On the other hand, we do not have access to the scene of his death. We do not have access to the witnesses. They cannot be cross-examined. The key witness, Al Hanashi himself, is dead.

With all the attention of the world upon Guantanamo, the actual events inside the Cuba-based U.S. prison are shrouded in deep mystery, sealed by classification and censorship. Hence the death of one man is barely known, much less remembered, and what happened to him even less known.

For the first time in this book, the circumstances around his death are open to public scrutiny. The record, even as it remains censored in part, shows that perceived violations of trust by doctors, nurses and mental health personnel contributed, at the very least, to Al Hanashi's decision to take his life. It is possible some person or persons – medical personnel or guards – facilitated his death, or even murdered Al Hanashi. We can only speculate.

"Everything seemed normal"

Al Hanashi had been suffering from depression and suicidal thoughts for some time. A long-time hunger striker, Al Hanashi's weight had fluctuated dramatically over the years, as detailed above. As a reminder, according to government records, on July 22, 2006 his weight dropped under 80 pounds. Only months before he had weighed just over 140. His weight had dropped by over 60 pounds in just four months.

According to his autopsy report, Al Hanashi had gone on hunger strike again in January 2009. During his last hunger strike, Al Hanashi was fed via tube. At his death, he weighed 120 lbs.

A Medical Record Review by NCIS investigators stated he entered the BHU on Jan. 10 for "making suicidal ideations." His autopsy report also noted that Al Hanashi had made five suicide attempts in the month before he died. The NCIS Medical Record Review contradicted that account, stating it was three attempts, all in the presence of prison personnel. By any account, Al Hanashi was deeply depressed and suicidal. Yet despite his history of recent suicide attempts, on the night he supposedly killed himself, Al Hanashi did not appear to be on suicide watch.

The guards reported little of consequence that evening. There were nine guards and a Watch Commander on duty that night, and seven detainees present on the BHU. One guard told NCIS investigators, "The BHU houses detainees that have expressed the desire to harm themselves."

The procedure on the unit was to have two guards at a time monitor the seven detainees. One African-American guard with the Naval Expeditionary Guard Battalion (NEGB) described the scene: "Our duties were to look inside each cell and check on the welfare of the detainees. We look inside the cell windows to ensure the detainees are not in possession of contraband or attempting to do harm to themselves. We usually spend approximately thirty seconds to one minute looking inside of each cell window."

For whatever reason, this guard changed his statement later to reflect the fact that guards only spent "approximately ~~thirty~~ few seconds ~~to one minute~~" watching the prisoner. The words "thirty" and "to one minute" were crossed out, though not enough that one couldn't see what was originally written.

"Everything seemed normal," the Navy guard stated. "I did not notice anything out of the ordinary.

Al Hanashi was in cell two and "seemed in good spirits." He had seen Al Hanashi upset in his cell before, pacing, or "praying loudly." He was not writing anything, the guard said, "or doing anything out of his normal pattern."

Another guard, who ended his roving tier patrol an hour before Al Hanashi died, told NCIS he too experienced the night as "normal." On the other hand, he did see Al Hanashi writing something for most of the time he was on his shift.

In addition, Al Hanashi did not seem "in good spirits" to this guard, but rather seemed "down." Al Hanashi was "a little more quiet than normal." Al Hanashi reportedly was "usually talkative." Nearly a full page of this guard's statement is still redacted and "under classification review" by a Command other than NCIS.

An African-American Navy Airman assigned to the BHU Response Team told NCIS about earlier contact with Al Hanashi.

It was mid-May, only a few weeks before Al Hanashi's death. He was told before his shift in mid-May 2009 that Al Hanashi had made a suicide attempt earlier that day. He'd rammed his head into a fence, and then tried to hang himself with his t-shirt.

The NCIS review of medical records dates the attempt to May13, and expanded on the story. Al Hanashi reportedly "slammed his head on an exposed bolt located on a fence in the BHU recreational area." The same day, he "attempted to strangle himself with a shirt."

Five days before the May 13 attempt, Al Hanashi had also "tore off pieces of his shirt and attempted to strangle himself in the recreation yard."

The guard told NCIS what he saw on his shift later that day after the suicidal behaviors, "Due to his suicide attempts, [redacted, but certainly 078, i.e., Al Hanashi] was under constant monitoring by a guard and he was placed in a green self harm suit. During the shift, [redacted, again, certainly 078] had some type of a Code Yellow (urgent medical issue) that required the response team to enter his cell and move him to the padded restraint chair adjacent to the tier."

The medical issue isn't known, but the guard thought, "[It] didn't seem to be serious." But another guard, in a different context, explained that Code Yellow means a detainee is "unresponsive."

Another guard, who was on tier duty on the Duty Section One (Nights) shift the day Al Hanashi died, also described his duties. "Our job on the tier is to check every detainee every three minutes," he told NCIS investigators. A check was only deemed satisfactory if they saw "breathing or some type of movement on each detainee."

That night, this guard heard Al Hanashi talking from his cell with other prisoners on the BHU. This was not unusual, but as the conversations were in Arabic, he didn't know what was said. There was nothing else unusual, either. Al Hanashi "seemed to be acting normal."

"Is he breathing"?

Later that night, around 9:45 pm, Al Hanashi asked the guard to get him the nurse on duty. He called a corpsman, who then called the nurse. The guard observed the nurse talk with Al Hanashi for 5 or 10 minutes. She left and came back shortly with a sleeping pill (though the guard didn't know what kind of pill it was at the time, he said). The guard watched him take it, swallowing it with water.

This guard heard Al Hanashi continue to talk to someone. The identity of the person he was speaking with is redacted in the documents, but from internal evidence it seems to have been the nurse. The last reported contact with Al Hanashi, according to the autopsy narrative, was 10-15 minutes after Al Hanashi spoke to the nurse who gave him the pill. "... [H]e asked the guard to close the 'bean hole cover,' a sign that he was ready to go to sleep."

Three minutes after his last check, "at approximately 2200," he looked inside the cell and "did not see any movement or breathing." Al Hanashi was described as lying "in the fetal position on the floor with the top of his head against the door and his feet facing the rear of his cell." A green blanket covered his body up to his eyes. His hair, hands and feet were sticking out.

"I am not involved in [redacted, likely '078's'] death," the guard told NCIS, somewhat defensively it seems.

Yet another guard, a Caucasian male with NEGB, was coming on duty right at the time Al Hanashi was discovered on the floor of his cell. He overheard the two guards who were checking on Al Hanashi's cell say "something to the effect, 'is he breathing' or 'check to see if he is breathing.'"

This guard looked in the room and Al Hanashi wasn't moving. He saw a woman, possibly a nurse, "dealing" with another detainee. She told the guard Al Hanashi might not be responding "because he had been given sleep medication by medical personnel." At the same time, two other detainees "began shouting that [redacted] was sleeping and that we should leave him alone."

The guard decided to ignore the warnings. He called in through a slot in the door to get Al Hanashi's attention. Another guard reached in through the lower slot in the door and tried to shake Al Hanashi, who was lying close to the door. But then something caught the guard's attention.

Al Hanashi was wearing a tan tee-shirt. (The autopsy described it as a khaki shirt.) "He was not authorized to wear a tee-shirt so the white fabric around his neck caught my attention. I called out that he had something around his neck and called a medical emergency," the guard told NCIS. Astonishingly, the NCIS investigator never commented on the unauthorized tee-shirt, nor did he or she ask any follow-up question. Everything at Guantanamo was thought out, was analyzed, and had meaning. The provision of clothes was no exception.

It would later turn out the ligature around his neck came from cotton briefs, but that doesn't change the fact that Al Hanashi was not wearing authorized clothing, or that the clothing he was wearing could be used to harm himself. BHU and guard staff evidently knew that very well. Only a few weeks before, on May 8, he had tried to hang himself with a tee-shirt while in the BHU recreation yard. As a result, afterward he was forced to wear self-harm prevention clothing, at least for a while.

The Nurse He Felt Betrayed His Trust

There was one nurse who Al Hanashi liked on the Behavioral Health Unit. Her name is unknown, but I will call her, for sake of narrative flow, Nurse "Friendly."

She knew Al Hanashi for only six weeks, but he reportedly favored her above others on the unit. She reminded him fondly of a female relative back in Yemen. Al Hanashi told her he enjoyed their conversations. She seemed to act kindly towards him. She was someone who inspired confidences.

Nurse "Friendly" told NCIS investigators that she spoke with many patients "for at least a couple minutes each shift to evaluate their mental state and physical condition." The night he died, she said she didn't see anything "suspicious" regarding Al Hanashi. She saw no one enter his cell, neither staff nor another detainee. She saw no signs of "foul play."

The nurse told NCIS that Al Hanashi told her "on several occasions" that he was "scared of being sent back to Yemen."

"Al Hanashi feared that he and his family would be tortured if he was returned to Yemen," Nurse "Friendly" told an NCIS investigator.

Four or five times Al Hanashi asked her to give him "a fix," i.e., "to give him a medication that would kill him." The nurse would ask follow-up questions to determine his seriousness, but she said he "always 'laughed it off.'" Even so,

Nurse "Friendly" reported the conversations to the Chief of the BHU, and to the guard force.

The request for assistance in suicide was no laughing matter. As already described, less than a month before he died, Al Hanashi tried to hang himself in the BHU recreation yard, and when that didn't work, ran his head into a metal fence bolt. Later, after his death, the autopsy examiner would note the presence of "a small cluster of dark raised lesions" on his Al Hanashi's forehead.

Even more, the medical examiner said the lesions were "consistent with [a] reported history of witnessed repeated self-inflicted [sic] hitting/banging of the head on detention facility walls." None of the released statements by guards or medical personnel allude to this history of demonstrated agony, although the autopsy report did mention Al Hanashi's history of "self-inflicted sharp force injuries and frequent blunt force trauma to the head."

The medical examiner also described a long history of "multiple suicide attempts by multiple modalities," going back to the second year of his incarceration. To the doctors, psychologists and mental health workers in the Guantanamo Behavioral Health Unit, Al Hanashi suffered from adjustment disorder and anti-social personality disorder.

They also wrote he suffered from "conditions of confinement." The euphemism was telling. They plied their medical and therapeutic wares in an atmosphere of torture and abuse, and they never could say, and possibly never could allow themselves to think the unthinkable. Unlike anti-social personality and adjustment disorders, "conditions of confinement" is not a diagnosis recognized in the psychiatric literature. It seems to be a paraphrase for torture.

The International Committee of the Red Cross (ICRC) found as early as June 2003 that the conditions of confinement at Guantanamo were "tantamount to torture," as was documented in a "Memorandum for the Record to Major General Geoffrey Miller" on October 8, 2003. Questions about psychological torture at the Navy base prison were raised by ICRC as early as the previous January. According to a New York Times article by

Neil Lewis, "the Red Cross team found a far greater incidence of mental illness produced by stress than did American medical authorities, much of it caused by prolonged solitary confinement."[85]

The stressors of confinement at Guantanamo are many, and include the anxiety and tension associated with indefinite detention, isolation, long bouts of intense interrogation, behavioral controls of reward and punishment, periods of sleep deprivation, lack of access for years to an attorney, separation from family and loved ones, cruel treatment and at times torture.

So it was a likely with a leap of special trust that Al Hanashi attempted to take Nurse "Friendly" into his confidence. A few weeks before he died, he asked her to meet him on the tier at noon on June 10. He asked her to promise she wouldn't tell anyone about it "or there would be 'big problems'." When she explained she could not keep such a promise regarding confidentiality, he became "agitated." Perhaps in an effort to placate him, or maybe she was being sincere, Nurse "Friendly" then told Al Hanashi she would "make every effort" to meet him on the time and date and the location he requested. But, she told NCIS investigators, Al Hanashi wouldn't say why the time and date were so important to him.

The next morning, she told the Chief at BHU about the conversation. He told NCIS interviewers that he didn't realize right away the significance of the June 10 date. Only later did he find out it was the anniversary of the 2006 "suicides."

On June 1, 2008, Nurse "Friendly" came to work already aware the BHU Chief had "confronted" Al Hanashi about the June 10 assignation and its significance. The Chief didn't say what Al Hanashi told him, though that might have been censored in the documents. As Nurse "Friendly" started her shift, she fully expected Al Hanashi would want to talk with her about what he perceived as a breach of confidentiality and trust by telling BHU authorities about his request.

At 2110 (8:10pm) Nurse "Friendly" went to talk to Al Hanashi in his cell. She brought him his medications – Klonopin, Benadryl, and Lactulose [the latter for constipation]. "[H]e asked her why she had informed [redacted, but probably the Chief] about their conversation relative to the meeting on June 10th." She told him "she was required as a part of her job to provide all information about possible patient safety issues to the BHU staff."

He "seemed fine after her explanation," Nurse "Friendly told NCIS investigators. Subsequent events proved how wrong she was.

Nurse "Friendly" was not the only medical staff, besides therapists, Al Hanashi confided in. In May 2009, in one of the episodes in the BHU recreation yard, when Al Hanashi "utilized his undershirt as a tourniquet around his neck in an attempt to choke himself," he was tended to by the Senior Medical Officer (SMO) to the Joint Medical Group at the Detention Hospital. The SMO was a woman, a 1996 Naval Academy graduate.

She told NCIS investigators how she responded to the scene in the Recreation Yard, and found Al Hanashi "had already been placed on a backboard." There was "redness around his neck from the tourniquet," and concerned medical staff took him for x-rays. Speaking through a camp linguist, Al Hanashi told the SMO that he "was very unhappy." Because he was at that point in the Detention Hospital, she saw that he was given a can of Ensure via a feeding tube. That was the last contact she had with Al Hanashi before he died.

The Psychologist

Because of the fragmentary nature of the available evidence, and the confusion wrought by censorship, it is sometimes difficult to know our dramatis personae with assurance. In his final statement – referred to by Guantanamo linguists as a "suicide note" – Al Hanashi explained he was upset that the general camp rules would be enforced from now on in the Behavioral Health Unit, and he turned to the BHU psychologist for help.

So far as I can tell, because their narratives match in crucial essentials, this psychologist was also, according to his own statement to NCIS, the Chief of Behavioral Health Services for Joint Task Force, Guantanamo. Not much is known about him, besides the fact he was African-American. He arrived at Guantanamo only on April 27, 2009, and was promoted to Chief "after a brief period of turnover." His assignment included providing "inpatient, outpatient, and consultative mental health services for all the detainees at the JTF camps." [86]

The Chief started treating Al Hanashi on May 10. He was briefed on his new patient. Detainee 078 was said to be a "leader among the detainees on the tier," thereby confirming for us something a former detainee, Binyam Mohamed, told the press after Al Hanashi died. According to the Chief, "the guard force was working with him to get input on detainee recreation and television schedules. He seemed to enjoy doing this."

Yet three days after he started working with the Chief, Al Hanashi butted his head into a metal fence, cutting his head, and then he tried to hang himself in the recreation yard with his t-shirt. The guards stopped him. Someone (whose identity was redacted by NCIS) told the Chief that Al Hanashi, who had made multiple attempts, always did so in the presence of guards or medical staff. As a result, the Chief told NCIS investigators that, despite his unpredictable behavior, "I considered his risk of suicide to be low."

The use of a tee-shirt as a noose recalls the statement by a Guantanamo guard that when he saw Al Hanashi motionless in his cell the night he died, he was surprised to see him wearing a tee-shirt as he was "was not authorized to wear a tee-shirt." No wonder. Yet, he was wearing one. Why?

A nurse described the head-banging incident as Al Hanashi deliberately "slamming" his head on a fence bolt. If anything, the Chief's version seemed to downplay the seriousness of the incident. Still, Al Hanashi was placed on suicide watch and made to wear a suicide smock, a garment made specifically to frustrate the attempts of users to render it into something one could use to hang or strangle oneself.

Al Hanashi told the Chief after the event that he was angry with him. The Chief said his patient told him he felt the Chief had not responded to his needs "in a timely manner." The Chief decided this suicidal behavior was another attempt to get attention, in this case, his attention.

When the Chief first arrived at the BHU, Al Hanashi was on a hunger strike. He reportedly was taking the feeding tube voluntarily. Two weeks after the Chief took over his treatment, Al Hanashi supposedly ended his hunger strike. The clinical staff saw this as "a sign of progress."

Al Hanashi had trouble opening up in psychological treatment with the Chief. The psychologist head of JTF-Gitmo's Behavioral Health Services felt this was normal. It was hard to transition from your old therapist, the Chief opined to NCIS investigators. Still, the Chief felt that Al Hanashi had been "warming up" to him over the month he saw him. Al Hanashi spoke of his fears about returning to Yemen someday, and of possible safety issues there for himself and his family. (He had said much the same thing to Nurse "Friendly.") The Chief referred him to the Staff Advocate's Office for follow-up. Al Hanashi supposedly seemed less anxious about the Yemen issue after the referral.

Al Hanashi also spoke about the 2006 suicides. According to the Chief's account, he "seemed to carry some guilt because he stated that he was supposed to be a part of the suicide." Somehow, in a way the Chief felt was obscure or never expressed, Al Hanashi was told not to kill himself. The entire episode seems possibly delusional on Al Hanashi's part, though in his statement and in medical records there is no indication that he had delusions of any sort. He had been given antipsychotic medication, specifically Haldol, but that was presumably for agitation. The full medical records have not been made available.

In addition, there is no written record by Al Hanashi himself that he felt he would have or should have died in June 2006 with the other three detainees. Since guards said that Al Hanashi often wrote at night, it's likely Guantanamo authorities had quite a collection of his writings. According to notes NCIS made on the translation of his "last will and testament" and "suicide note," Al Hanashi's handwritten notes had been collected at his own request and stored in a blue folder in the Behavioral Health Unit.

According to the Chief, "The entire medical staff provided him therapy to try and reduce his guilt." No progress notes or other types of psychotherapy or clinical notes have been made available to back up this assertion. In any case, Al Hanashi seemed to respond to the treatment, the Chief thought, though he couldn't be sure.

Then, on Memorial Day weekend, May 23 or 24, 2009, Nurse "Friendly" told the Chief about Al Hanashi's request that he meet with her on the BHU tier on June 10, the third anniversary of the deaths of the three detainees. She told the Chief that she tried to get more information from Al Hanashi about why he wanted to meet with her, but had no luck. The Chief reported that he had to research the significance of the date. Somehow, it seems unlikely he did not know about that anniversary, and if he didn't, that itself is a kind of indictment about how aloof and indifferent major elements of health staff were to camp conditions.

In any case, the Chief said that once he did understand the significance, he went to "JTF medical and detention leadership." *They* were "well aware" of the pending anniversary date. Even so, because Al Hanashi had made no specific statements threatening self-harm, the Chief explained, "we continued to care for his needs the same way we managed the other detainees on the tier." The Chief therefore ignored the fact that the request to Nurse "Friendly" came contemporaneously with a spate of suicidal behavior. This seems obtuse, at best.

Hence, though it was only ten days or so from his last suicide attempt, itself the second in the past previous two weeks or so, Guantanamo Behavioral Health Unit clinical staff took no extra safety precautions for their patient Al Hanashi, so far as we know. (Of course, there is that guard's statement that Al Hanashi should not have had a tee-shirt.) "We remained aware of the upcoming anniversary date" for the 2006 "suicides," the Chief told NCIS, and they presumably thought that was enough.

We have seen how the guards subsequently looked in on Al Hanashi, how he asked to see a nurse, how he was given a nighttime sedative, and then subsequently the discovery of his body, the attempts at medical resuscitation, and the declaration of death.

While the NCIS investigation into Al Amri's death was closed in a little over a year, the investigation into Al Hanashi's death took 3-1/2 years. It seems likely the investigation into the DIMS shutdown lengthened the time of investigation. There may have been other reasons as well. Just as we don't know who ordered the computer database recording shutdown upon Al Hanashi's death, it seems we may never know exactly how or why he died.

Chapter 5
The Mysterious Death of Abdul Rahman Al Amri

In the summer of 2015, I received a response to a three-year old FOIA request from the Naval Criminal Investigative Service (NCIS) on its investigation into the death of Abdul Rahman Al Amri in May 2007. Little did I know then that someone else had made a similar FOIA request in October 2009 on the "suicide" of "Al Amry." I don't know who made it, or whatever happened to that particular request. But when I got my initial tranche of records, I discovered that out of an apparent 584 pages, NCIS had released only 11 percent, or 63 pages, while withholding hundreds of pages "for classification review." Meanwhile, even the 63 pages released were heavily redacted.

According to his JTF GTMO Detainee Assessment released by Wikileaks[87], Al Amri, labeled ISN 199 by prison authorities, was "a member of Al Qaida, probably with a leadership role." He was born in 1973 in Saudi Arabia, and served approximately nine years in the Saudi army, where his brother was a colonel. He reportedly trained with U.S. forces and learned to use various U.S. made weapons, including the Tow and Dragon anti-tank missiles. Intelligence officials felt his "extensive military training… added to his worth in the Al-Qaida organization."

According to the U.S. government narrative, Al Amri left the Saudi army in 2000, and became interested in fighting on behalf of the Taliban. Indeed, according to his unsworn statement given via his Guantanamo-provided "personal representative" to the Combatant Status Review Tribunal (CSRT) set up by the Bush Administration at Guantanamo, he "stated it was his duty to fight for Jihad."[88]

According to his Detainee Assessment, Al Amri had "ties to many Al Qaida leaders." Guantanamo intelligence officials insisted he knew of the 9/11 attacks in advance, and was even recruited to Al Qaida by one of the 9/11 hijackers. Hence, he was considered a "high risk" to U.S. interests, and a "high threat from a detention perspective."

The "evidence" of Al Amri's foreknowledge of 9/11 evidently came from an interrogation on February 15, 2002, only six days after he arrived in Guantanamo. Since many interrogations at Guantanamo were tainted by abuse and torture, one wonders how much credence one can give to the confessions regarding 9/11 foreknowledge or recruitment by a hijacker. By the time he had his CSRT tribunal, there was no mention of 9/11 at all.

Perhaps one reason was that government interrogators had declared that Al Amri stated that the killings on 9/11 of civilians made him "very upset." The particulars of the charge that he had foreknowledge of the 9/11 attacks (and Al Amri apparently did know of some attack but not the particulars) came from a Saudi detainee, Abd Al Aziz Abd Al Rahman (ISN 264), whose DoD detainee record showed a history of "anxiety and depression with transient psychotic symptoms."[89] He was a self-mutilator who had been in Guantanamo's BHU. The mental health issues by themselves don't mean Al Rahman was not trustworthy, but it opens up the possibility that he was coerced into statements, or said under the stress of captivity, if not torture, what he thought his captors wanted to hear.

Pakistani forces captured Al Amri after fleeing with others from the battle at Tora Bora in late December 2001. He was turned over to U.S. forces on New Years Eve.

Al Amri didn't deny having seen various Al Qaeda figures in Afghanistan, including Osama bin Laden. "In many instances it was a normal part of the processes and places in Afghanistan," he told CSRT officials.

The government accounts are not without their vagaries. For instance, according to the CSRT record, Al Amri supposedly came to Afghanistan in September 2001, but his Detainee Assessment reports he arrived in January 2001. Al

Amri told CSRT officials he came to Afghanistan in September 2000.

Al Amri said he went under an alias in Afghanistan: Abu Anas. This apparently led to his being "identified as the person responsible for providing a movie that provided all the details on how the USS Cole was attacked and the explosives that were used." The USS Cole was bombed on October 12, 2000 in the Yemen port of Aden, killing 17 sailors and injuring 39 more. Today, Abd al-Rahim al-Nashiri is held at Guantanamo's Camp 7, awaiting trial for planning the bombing. During his years in CIA captivity, Al Nashiri was tortured, including waterboarding.

Al Amri denied he had anything to do with the Cole bombing, and said he made no video about it. He told the CSRT tribunal he only had a middle school education. He indicated that he had been in the rear lines at Tora Bora, and his goal was to escape to Pakistan. He denied he had any intent to harm Americans.

Al Amri's CSRT statement notes, "Detainee said had his desire been to fight and kill Americans, he could have done that while he was side by side with them in Saudi Arabia."

Once in Guantanamo, Al Amri would have been subjected to all the in-processing procedures of other detainees, including being flown to Guantanamo with a scopolamine patch behind his ear, and given a treatment dose of 1200 mg (in divided doses) of mefloquine soon upon arrival.

According to the Detainee Assessment, he twice participated in hunger strikes, in 2003 and 2005. Camp authorities force-fed him. The record of his hunger strikes, recorded by his prisoner number, ISN 199, can plausibly be read in the Department of Defense release of Guantanamo detainee weight measurements.[90] The measurements can seem flaky, and it is possible that mistakes in data entry were sometimes made. Still, the measurements show Al Amri entered Guantanamo at weight 150. In June 2003, he still weighed 148, but by November 2, 2003, he was down to 125. Yet a week later, on November 9, he's said to be back up to 139.6 pounds. Could this have been due to forced feeding?

Other dramatic fluctuations occur. In August 2004 he's said to weigh 140 pounds. But by December 2004 he was at 115, a drop of 25 pounds. Then, a month later, in January 2005, he's recorded as weighing 160 pounds, an even more incredible weight gain of 45 pounds in one month! From February through May 2004, the record notes Al Amri refused the weighing procedure. He did so again in September and October of the same year.

By May 12, 2005, he supposedly was weighing 92 pounds. At his June 2005 weighing he's at 157.6. On July 11, 2005, during a time of widespread hunger striking at Guantanamo, he weighed 100.1 pounds, yet only three weeks later he'd gained almost 27 pounds.

By late September 2005 or early October, his weight had taken a definite nosedive down to the 90s, reaching a nadir of 89.1 pounds on November 28, 2005, during a period of assumed hunger striking. But given the wild gyrations of his weight, either for some period the measurements were terribly off, or the forced feeding was at times filling Al Amri with added weight far beyond what was necessary for survival.

Certainly, many detainees saw the food situation at Guantanamo as unpalatable, if not punishing. Australian David Hicks wrote about it in book, <u>Guantanamo: My Story</u>:

"Events like mealtimes in a prison setting are usually looked forward to because it breaks the monotony and gives one something to do for a short period, in addition to satisfying hunger. But food itself had become a form of punishment. Meals such as green, powdered scrambled eggs would be served along with oranges so extremely freezer burnt that no moisture was left. Hard-boiled eggs were first cooked and de-shelled on the U.S. mainland, deep-frozen and reheated months later at Guantanamo, leaving the whites the consistency of leather. All hot meals were cooked in thick oil, and if they were served cold the entire meal solidified into a single gooey conglomerate. In Camp Six, the soldiers used to put our hot meals in front of a large air-conditioner duct for a couple of hours before serving, which made it practically inedible. Not even the simplest pleasure was allowed to relieve us from the constant hardship, but only used to exacerbate. Even today, if I could, I would just take a nutrition pill and be done with it."[91]

At some point after it opened, Al Amri was sent to the then-new Camp 5 facility. According to an Amnesty International spokesperson's remarks upon Al Amri's death, the high-security prison at Camp 5 "created even harsher and apparently more permanent conditions of extreme isolation and sensory deprivation" than previous camp facilities.[92]

When the news broke of Al Amri's death, Miami Herald reporter Carol Rosenberg reported that the "means" of the detainee's death had "long been of interest" (but to whom she didn't say). More importantly, she wrote, "... prison camp tours for media and distinguished visitors emphasize that Camp Five is designed with suicide proofing such as towel hooks that won't bear the weight of a detainee, to prevent him from hanging himself."

"Moreover," Rosenberg continued, "the tours emphasize that each captive, housed in single-occupancy cell, is under constant Military Police and electronic monitoring, which means a guard is supposed to look in on him at least every three minutes."[93] In other words, Al Amri could not have had the time to construct the noose and thread it through the tiny holes of the air vent grating, tie his hands behind his back and then hang himself until all his life was gone out of him without being seen by anybody.

* * * *

Whatever Al Amri's level of compliance, or the truth about his history with Al Qaida, he was never charged with any crimes. He also never saw an attorney. During his stay at Guantanamo, he apparently was in poor health, suffering from chronic Hepatitis B and various musculoskeletal ailments and pains. Ironically, his JTF GTMO formal assessment describes his health problems while still proclaiming he was in "good health."

A separate report from a detainee who knew Al Amri was given to his attorney, Candace Gorman, in July 2007. Libyan detainee Abdul Hamid al-Ghizzawi told Gorman that, like himself, Al Amri suffered from Hepatitis B and tuberculosis. He also claimed that both he and Al Amri had not been treated for their ailments.

Gorman wrote, "Al-Ghizzawi, now so sick he can barely walk, told me that Amri, too, had been ill and then, suddenly, he was dead.

"Al-Ghizzawi also mentioned that Amri had engaged in hunger strikes in the past but had stopped a long time ago because of his health."[94]

Like so many Guantanamo prisoners, the true story of what Al Amri endured in Guantanamo is lost, or buried in classified reports, or left for us to piece together from records such as those on his weight, or the few reports from prisoners like al-Ghizzawi. Al Amri's own voice is necessarily conspicuously absent from this account.

One exception to the general fog surrounding the circumstances of Al Amri's incarceration comes from a September 2007 story by Ben Fox at Associated Press.[95] Fox reported that in an April 2002 interrogation, that is, some few months after arriving in Guantanamo, Al Amri told interrogators (or possibly Guantanamo authorities themselves) that detainees were feeling desperate, that they had "nothing to lose," and guards should take precautions in regards to possible suicide attempts.

Fox said the information came from a government report, which was "among thousands of pages of documents obtained by the AP... under the Freedom of Information Act."

According to this government report, "The detainee was aware that some detainees felt that they would rather die than live the way they were living, and some of the detainees would not care about taking someone else with them when they die."

The Ben Fox article also mentioned a separate document, a 2005 review of Al Amri's detention, more specifically, a "Summary of Evidence" (SOE) for DoD's Office for the Administrative Review of the Detention of Enemy Combatants.[96] The SOE report noted that Al Amri told interrogators that he had been a "heavy hashish and heroin user," but that he tired of that life and became more religious in the late 1990s. He went on the Hajj in 2000, and later, influenced by a religious scholar in Saudi Arabia, decided to go to fight jihad for the Taliban in Afghanistan. When he stopped using drugs, the report said, his "friends were amazed at his life change."

The SOE said Al Amri was a "very cooperative" prisoner, which seems to be corroborated by the other report Ben Fox referenced which described the Saudi detainee warning Guantanamo authorities of possible camp suicides. Al Amri even said (reportedly) that he was nervous because he was seen talking so often to interrogators. He feared other detainees "will think he is helping the Americans."

Reports of Al Amri's cooperativeness don't seem consistent with his participation in hunger strikes. This is another mystery about the narrative record of what really happened inside Guantanamo that probably could only be solved by a full release of all documents, and the ability to independently interview all staff and detainees, something that only a government inquiry with full subpoena powers would be able to implement. The likelihood of such an inquiry grows dimmer by the year.

According to Al Amri's autopsy report, quietly released in 2012, slipped into a document dump responsive to an ACLU FOIA lawsuit, he was found dead in his cell, hanging from a noose presumably cut from his bed sheets, and, surprisingly, with his hands tied behind his back.

The autopsy stated, "By report... fabric bound his hands loosely behind him." Later in the report, the examiner wrote, "There is no soft tissue evidence of recent binding around the wrists." This is evidently in reference to the hand-binding allegation. But according to the December 21, 2007 lab report, "Results of Evidence Analysis" by the U.S. Army Criminal Investigation Laboratory (USACIL) – part of the FOIA release – a short strip of purported bed-sheet that was used to bind Al Amri's hands was part of the evidence turned over to them for examination. The autopsy report, written before the evidence was examined by USACIL, never references the actual existence of the hand binding material.

In addition, in the NCIS materials released, there were statements by witnesses at the death scene and in Room 140 at Guantanamo's Camp 5, the medical room to which Al Amri was taken after he was found, that his hands were also bound with flex cuffs after he was first discovered in his cell. So there is no question that his hands were indeed bound, both before and after his death. But who took off the cloth bindings? It makes sense they were removed by guards in order to allow the placement of the flex cuffs. How did the cloth bindings make their way to the lab? We don't know, as no statements relating to that have yet been released.

The entire mystery takes on an added element of doubt when the FOIA records also reveal that some of the evidence from the death scene, notably another strip from the bed sheet, was apparently thrown into medical waste and lost forever. We know this from the USACIL lab report and from some off-hand comments from witness statements that NCIS neglected to censor.

This is the key section from NCIS's report on the USACIL analysis of evidence (bold added for emphasis):

"On 21NOV07, Reporting Agent (RA) received the results of the evidence analysis.... In the findings report produced by the USACIL, paragraph 4 (page 2) mentions a telephone call with RA. In the telephone call between RA and [redacted two to four words] Forensic Chemist USACIL, [redacted] informed RA that **it appeared a small piece(s) of the [bed] sheet was missing**, preventing a full reconstruction of the sheet. At this time RA advised [redacted] that subsequent to submission to USACIL, it was determined that **an additional small piece of sheet was also in evidence (MPGT Log number 034-07, Item D). This small piece of sheet had been used to bind the hands of V/AL UMARI**. Additionally, RA informed [redacted] that **a second small piece of sheet, similar in size to the hand binding, was reportedly discarded with medical waste items, prior to NCIS' arrival on scene.**

[Redacted] opined that those two pieces could have completed the sheet."

"*Could* have completed the sheet"? Weren't they sure? And why would a piece of evidence have been thrown away? At one point, a medical witness who had been present at the scene in Room 140, where CPR was being fruitlessly applied to Al Amri, told NCIS investigators that likely there was so much activity in the room, the cloth material was accidently tossed. But what if the cloth material were, like the rags shoved down the throats of the 2006 detainees also found dead in their cells a year earlier, used to "dryboard" or gag the prisoner?[97]

We'll return to this missing "small piece of sheet" further along. But it's worth noting here that in the Seton Hall investigation of the 2006 detainee deaths, Denbeaux and his team found that NCIS had suppressed a document from Master of Arms Denny, who was at Guantanamo that night. He told investigators he had seen a Corpsman wrap an altered detainee sheet around the wrist of one detainee, Yasser Talal al Zahrani. The cloth matched the ligature around al Zahrani's throat.

"The cloth was not on the detainees [sic] wrists when the Camp 1 guards removed the handcuffs a few minutes earlier," Denny testified. But the "fact" that all the "suicides" had their hands bound was supposed to be evidence of use of simultaneous suicide as "asymmetrical warfare." Denny's account shows the "evidence" was being fabricated *after* the supposed suicides themselves.[98] Was a similar frame-up being contemplated in the case of Al Amri? Is this why the Officer in Charge at Camp 5 would tell NCIS investigators that there were concerns of "possible additional suicide attempts" that night, as is described in greater length below?

Complicating the puzzle of how Al Amri actually died is the fact that it appears NCIS intervened to limit the scientific examination of the evidence in the case, and in at least one instance was lax about pursuing relevant evidence.

According to the USACIL report, lab technicians concluded (bold added), "all fabric items discovered in V/AL UMARI's cell could have originated from the bed sheet issued to V/AL UMARI **or a similar source**." If the material did not originate from Al Amri's bed sheet, then what other "similar source" did it originate? Could it have been a sheet used by someone else to fabricate the materials for the detainee's presumed hanging? Wouldn't one think they would have tried to nail the origin of the killing ligature down?

The Army lab apparently thought it worth pursuing, but was stopped. The USACIL report explains it had Al Amri's sheet, the rope made from sheet-like material, and pieces of the rope attached to the grating by which Al Amri was found hanging. Technicians found "no significant differences" between these rope pieces and a control sheet provided to them by authorities. The "control sheet" was supposed to be the same as the sheet supplied to Al Amri.

The lab's conclusion was the pieces of fabric from Al Amri's cell *could* all originate from a single or similar source. But no further tests were run to determine if they actually did originate from a sheet such as Al Amri's. The report states, "Due to circumstances of this case and per telephone conversation with SA MCCARVER, no further comparisons of Exhibits 2 and 4 [that is, the rope or the pieces of rope attached to the grating] to Exhibit 6 [the control sheet for comparison purposes] were conducted."

It's unclear what is meant by the "circumstances of the case," or why that would mean less clarity regarding results would be desirable. You would think that a death at Guantanamo, particularly after all the publicity of the 2006 deaths, was something whose circumstances would entail every lead be pursued and explained. But instead, the record on the investigation into Al Amri's death shows the opposite. Leads are not pursued, and relevant evidence, as in the case of other Guantanamo detainees (like Al Hanashi and Latif, as described elsewhere in this book) goes missing.

Perhaps it was enough that on first examination there were "no significant differences" between the hanging rope and the sample sheet. But that was not all. The rope and manipulated sheet materials all had "[f]oreign hairs and other miscellaneous debris" on them. The lab report noted flatly, ""No judgment as to the suitability of these hairs for examination has been made."

USACIL suggested, however, that if NCIS wanted a hair analysis done, it should contact USACIL, who would contract the work to "an external source."

But the "foreign hairs" were never examined, or at least there is no record of that in the materials NCIS released via FOIA. There is no reason to believe that such an analysis or its results would not have been released, particularly if the results were non-remarkable. If such an analysis was done, and results of significance withheld, that would be evidence of a cover-up. But as it is, we just don't know.

The failure to follow-up the evidence pertaining to the bed sheet and the rope and other bindings (or even gag) associated with it is replicated in the case of the razor that was purportedly used to cut the sheets. The piece of razor ostensibly used by Al Amri was marked Exhibit 3 by the examining lab. It was a broken piece of razor, 1/4 inch wide by 1" in length. "One end has a jagged edge and possibly broken," the lab report said. NCIS argued it originated from a disposable shaving razor, and submitted such a sample razor (Exhibit 5) to lab personnel for "control" purposes. A disposable razor was apparently provided to the detainees for shaving purposes.

But, according to the official 2004 Camp Delta "Standard Operating Procedures"[99] manual, razors were contraband items. Razors for shaving were allowed only during shower period, but guards were instructed to "Ensure the return of intact razors." No razors were issued to detainees. If detainees did shave, use of the razor was monitored "at all times." Moreover, detainees in "segregation" units, i.e., isolation, as was Al Amri, are not supposed to be issued razors during shower period at all, raising questions how he ever obtained a blade, if he did at all. If Al Amri did secure a razor, it seems it would be related to a significant breakdown in SOPs.

Moreover, as with the Hanashi's underwear, there was no attempt (that we know of, anyway) by NCIS to account for the missing portions of the item used to supposedly fashion a death-seeking tool. With Hanashi, there was a ligature made from underwear, but no leftover underwear. In the case of Al Amri, we have a portion of a razor blade, but no other part of the blade or razor itself. We have no way of knowing these things were provided or entered the cell from the outside, or by other persons involved.

The autopsy report gives no explanation as to how Al Amri obtained a razor blade. It does mention a "superficial, incised wound" on the forefingers of each of his hands, and these could have come from a razor, although the autopsy report does not conclude what their source is.

The idea that a contraband or dangerous article could have been placed in Al Amri's cell is not a paranoid fantasy by this author. In a May 25, 2010 letter to his attorneys, David Remes and Marc Falcoff, Guantanamo inmate Adnan Farhan Abdul Latif complained that camp authorities were denying him items he needed, like soap, eye glasses, pillow, etc. Instead, they were giving him items with which he could hurt himself.

Latif particularly mentioned "the person responsible for camp five" gave him a "big pair of scissors." "[T]hey want me to die and to kill me," Latif concluded.[100] Indeed, whether due to planning by Latif himself, lax policies on medication dispersal by camp hospital officials, or intended facilitation of suicide, Latif himself died of a drug overdose on September 8, 2012. Like Mohamed al Hanashi, he died while held in Guantanamo's BHU. His death is the subject of the next chapter in this book.

I want to briefly discuss the Al Amri case as an exemplar of the lies and cover-up that emanate from Guantanamo, and secondarily, as an example of the complicity of the press, who while they churn out commemorative pieces for dates like this latest anniversary, have shown (with a few exceptions) no appetite to really get to the truth of what was and is still is going on in that remote island prison. Current censorship policy includes, among other things, the classification of things detainees have said, and what attorneys have heard from them.

As was noted in a February 2012 story at the website Truthout on Al Amri's death[101], and that of another detainee, Mohammad Ahmed Abdullah Saleh Al Hanashi in June 2009, "Authorities consulted… agreed, as one source[102] put it, that having hands tied behind one's back in a hanging 'does not necessarily indicate homicide but certainly requires additional investigation.'"

But the Department of Defense never released publicly the fact that Al Amri - who DoD sometimes refers to in documents as Al Umari - was found with his hands bound, and while I broke the story that he was indeed discovered that way, no other member of the news media, or agency or institution that reports on detainee conditions ever saw fit to follow up on the story, or even report it. In the meantime, I filed a FOIA for the investigative reports on his death completed by NCIS, and for the Army's 15-6 statutory report on the death filed at Guantanamo's ruling headquarters, Southern Command (SOUTHCOM).

I had also asked for the toxicology report[103] on Al Amri's death, because according to his autopsy report[104], he had inexplicably been tested for the presence of the anti-malaria drug mefloquine after his death. This was very strange. While there is no malaria problem in Cuba, all incoming detainees were administered a full treatment dose of mefloquine (also known as Lariam) upon entry into the prison, for supposed prophylactic purposed, i.e., as a public health measure.

But even if the public health rationale were true - and Jason Leopold and I published a series[105] of articles[106] demonstrating that the use of the controversial drug mefloquine had likely nefarious purposes[107], or as one military doctor put it, constituted "pharmacologic waterboarding" - Al Amri had been in Guantanamo for five years, and there was no reason to assume mefloquine had been in his blood stream for years.

In fact, military laboratory tests found no mefloquine. The toxicology report on Al Amri, dated June 7, 2007, carried a separate paragraph for the mefloquine results: "No mefloquine was detected in the blood at a limit of quantitation of 0.01 mg/L using liquid chromatography/mass spectrometry."

One can only presume that *someone* thought he had possibly been administered mefloquine sometime in the period prior to his death, and then asked the Armed Forces Institute of Pathology to see if it was still present at the time of death itself.

The possibility of using such a drug, whose only purpose was prophylaxis or treatment of malaria, and which was already under tough criticism within DoD over its use on U.S. military personnel, raises serious questions regarding the purpose of administering that drug. Were mefloquine's side-effects of inducing dizziness, nausea and paranoia or hallucinations in some people being used to chemically torture detainees?

Even more perplexing... why would Al Amri tie his hands behind his back before killing himself? Did he in fact do so, or was he actually murdered in his cell by guards, or others? I had hoped the FOIA material on the investigations would answer some of these questions.

But when the materials arrived from the NCIS FOIA office last July, they were heavily censored. Even more, hundreds of pages were withheld in their entirety as supposedly consisting of "documents proprietary to another Command." I was told, "Those documents have been referred for a classification review and releasability determination and return to this office."

All told, approximately 500 pages from the investigation have been withheld, awaiting "classification review." From what was released, much is redacted.

NCIS would not tell me what other "Command" they were referring to: that was classified, too (although I highly suspect the other Command is JTF GTMO itself). I've also wondered if the other "Command" also included the CIA. Meanwhile, six months later, I'm still waiting for clearance of this huge section of the FOIA, which was originally filed in 2012.

As for the SOUTHCOM AR 15-6 investigation, that is still under classificatory review as well, and months away from release... if I'm lucky.

Such delay in the matter of a FOIA on a detainee's death is not always so protracted. Yemeni detainee Adnan Latif was found dead in his cell in the Behavioral Health Unit at Guantanamo in September 2012. His AR 15-6 report was released in a reasonable period after a FOIA request was filed (and was the basis of news reports in 2013, again, by both Jason Leopold[108] and myself[109]).

Is this because Al Amri died under even incredibly more suspicious circumstances than Latif? Not only did the USACIL investigators note the presence of the hand binding, they had, as described above, mentioned another missing piece of sheet that was reportedly similar in size to the hand binding. Whatever that piece of sheet was, it was apparently thrown away prior to NCIS's appearance on the scene.

"I don't recall throwing away any strips of sheet-like materials," an "Individual Augmentee" assigned to the Joint Medical Group told NCIS. He had been working at Camp 6, heard the Code Snowball, and then accompanied the Officer in Charge and the Senior Medical Officer to the Camp 5 Medical room where he saw Al Amri on his back on the exam table.

NCIS must have already been aware of the missing strip of fabric, as various witnesses interviewed spoke to their knowledge, or rather lack of knowledge, of what happened to that missing strip. Someone had to have seen it originally, and reported it, but the documentary record as we have it doesn't say who that was.

"Again, we cleaned up all the sharps, bagged up the trash, and took it with us," the Individual Augmentee told NCIS. "We then went to Camp 6 for debrief. I threw the trash away inside Camp 6 medical where they have a big trashcan."

Another statement, from a Black male assigned to Joint Medical Group, JTF-GTMO, and more particularly to the Behavioral Health Unit, told investigators, "I did not notice at any time any kind of hand restraints on the detainee. I also did not assist with the cleaning up of the medical room or disposal of any medical waste." For future reference, we will call this man the Assessor, for he claimed to have the assignment of "assess[ing] the mental status of detainees while they are in GTMO." He also told NCIS his job "includes assessing the detainee after a snowball or any code."

It seems highly likely this Assessor was actually a military psychologist assigned to the BHU, as his duties carried a serious responsibility in regards to the mental status or health of the detainees.

Finally, we have the testimony from the "Resuscitation Note" written by the Officer in Charge for the Joint Medical Group. He was a white male, and his report was dated June 5, 2007. At the close of the report is an "Addendum" (bold added for emphasis):

"At the time of my arrival on scene, **no wrist bindings or remnant of neck ligature were noted to be present on the body**. The medical scene quickly got very crowded and busy. **Pieces may have been present in medical waste.** The room was cleaned and re-stocked very quickly due to the concerns of possible additional suicide attempts and resuscitations."

"Concerns of possible additional suicide attempts"? Did the OIC and other Guantanamo officials anticipate a replay of the 2006 "suicides"? Threats of mass suicides went back to the early days of the camp.[110] Certainly the Al Amri death scene was very reminiscent of the scene surrounding the deaths of three prisoners a year earlier. All had been hunger strikers. All were reportedly found hanging. All were bound (though Al Amri had his hands bound behind him, unlike the 2006 corpses). Additionally, as regards the investigation of their deaths, all three who died in 2006, as well as Al Amri in 2007, were administered toxicology tests for the presence of the antimalarial drugs chloroquine and/or mefloquine.

The three 2006 bodies had been discovered with cloth rags of some sort shoved down their throats. This possible "dryboarding" of the prisoners may have been replicated in the case of Al Amri. While we have no report of any gagging or presence of cloth or rag in Al Amri's throat from any witness, the documentary record is, as described elsewhere, highly incomplete and censored. Moreover, while we do know that some piece of cloth was ostensibly thrown away that was part of the Al Amri death scene, and given the fact it was likely thrown away with medical waste in the Camp 5 Medical Room – that it was something found on his body – it seems plausible that it was in fact some kind of gagging or "dryboarding" cloth used to suffocate or gag Al Amri.

In the initial report of investigation by NCIS on Al Amri's death, dated May 31, 2007, the reporting agent notes that Al Amri was moved from his cell to Camp 5 Medical Room prior to NCIS arriving on the scene. But was NCIS present in the Medical Room itself? We don't know.

The initial narrative was simple enough. Al Amri was found hanging inside his cell in Bravo Block, Camp 5, at approximately 12:56 pm on May 30, 2007. The autopsy authorities imagined he had "likely stood on his bedroll to place the noose over his head."

He was discovered by guards, cut down, and placed on a backboard. He was then transported to Room 140, Camp 5's medical room. Medical personnel examined him. They "found he was not breathing, had no pulse, had bruising around the neck, no pupil reaction and had facial cyanosis." CPR was begun, but the detainee did not respond. The automated Defibrillator in the medical room never showed anything but "No Shock Indicated."

According to the official I've called the Assessor, at the medical room he saw Al Amri was wearing tan pants but no shirt or shoes. He noticed that he had urinated on himself. A woman, likely a nurse, but not absolutely identified in the fragmentary documentary record, initially told NCIS also that Al Amri was wearing a tan shirt. But the next day she officially changed her story and said she realized he was not wearing any shirt at all. She added, according to the NCIS Participating Agent who interviewed her, "she was not sure if there was anything around V/AL UMARI's neck. [Redacted] related this was her first response to death and she was mistaken in her earlier statement."[111]

Al Amri was pronounced dead about 40 minutes after he was found. Someone in Room 140 took down everyone's names. A debriefing took place in Camp 6, while an ambulance took the deceased to the Naval Hospital Guantanamo morgue. They covered his body with a white sheet.

Al Amri had other medical conditions, his records showed. He had Hepatitis B, Gastroesophageal Reflux Disease, and kidney stones. He supposedly had no mental health diagnosis. (I saw no reference to tuberculosis, which another detainee maintained Al Amri had.) The medical records in any case would remain in the possession of JTF-GTMO personnel. NCIS could look at them "at any time," but would not get material possession of the records.

NCIS received their referral for the investigation from a Staff Judge Advocate at Guantanamo. Soon thereafter, a Supervising Special Agent from NCIS provided an initial debrief for both the Commander and the Chief of Staff, JTF-GTMO.

After the initial flurry of NCIS interviews, and the referral of evidence analysis to USACIL, the investigation appreciably slowed. The interim report of investigation for November 21, 2007 states "no substantive investigative efforts have been expanded" since a previous report on Oct. 17.

By February 27, 2008, a Death Review Panel (DRP), which consisted of two Supervisory Special Agents, one Assistant Special Agent in Charge, and a Forensic Consultant, at NCIS South East Field Offices in Mayport, Florida, had reviewed the investigation and concluded it was ready for review by the NCIS Headquarters Death Review Board.

On July 9, 2008, the NCIS investigation into Al Amri's death was officially closed. Headquarters asked that the complete case file be submitted to it as "this investigation has a pending Freedom of Information Act request and expeditious handling is requested." If there was ever a release of such a FOIA request, I am unaware of it. In any case, no other public examination of the investigation into Al Amri's death has ever been published. We can assume, by the request for "expeditious handling," that the request came from someone in the press. Why no article ever came of it we will likely never know.

There were, at least initially, some calls for further investigation. Soon after Al Amri's death, according to a story in Arab News, the National Society for Human Rights in Saudi Arabia "called for an independent and neutral inquiry into the circumstances surrounding Al-Amri's death." The story noted the fact that Al Amri's death occurred even as the NCIS investigation to the 2006 "suicides" was still ongoing.[112]

According to another article in Arab News, a week after Al Amri's death, his relatives were highly dubious about the suicide verdict provided by the U.S. government. "'We did not find any marks on his body which would hint that he committed suicide,' said Muhammad Al-Amri, the deceased's brother."[113]

The article added, "Spokesperson for the Interior Ministry, Maj. Gen. Mansour Al-Turki, said that a special medical committee would do an autopsy and then prepare a report that will be sent to U.S. authorities on any particular inquires." But to my knowledge no such report has ever surfaced publicly. My request for comment by the Saudi Interior Ministry was never answered.

Chapter 6
Latif, Another Nightmarish Death at Guantanamo[114]

In response to a Freedom of Information request Jason Leopold filed with the Department of Defense, in June 2013 U.S. Southern Command released a redacted copy of an official Army Regulation 15-6 investigation into the "facts and circumstances" surrounding the death of Guantanamo detainee Adnan Farhan Abd Latif. After a number of stays in the prison's Behavioral Health Unit, Latif had been moved to Guantanamo's high-security Camp 5 when he reportedly killed himself by overdose on September 8, 2012.

The tenor of the report, which is dated November 8, 2012, is captured in the fact that after the report's first page, Latif is almost never referred to by name but only as a number: ISN156. This is in contrast to the NCIS material, where the deceased prisoners are referred to by the abbreviation "victim/[detainee's last name]." In all these cases, one is struck by the bureaucratic effects of isolating language that objectifies the deceased.

In addition, the Army authors practically never mention the stressors of indefinite detention, "forceful cell extractions" (beatings), isolation, and other forms of abuse and torture that Latif suffered. Meanwhile, camp medical authorities were quick to label the young traumatic brain injury victim as suffering from bipolar disorder, in addition to both borderline and antisocial personality disorders.

The government's criteria for diagnosing antisocial personality order does not follow the guidelines of the American Psychiatric Association's Diagnostic and Statistical Manual used in making diagnoses, in that there is no way that the government had information of the earlier presence of a conduct disorder in Latif before age 15. Such presence is necessary to diagnose antisocial personality disorder. According to the American Psychiatric Association's diagnostic manual, the diagnosis calls for the showing of a "pervasive pattern of disregard for and violation of the rights of others since age 15 years." It's clear the personality disorder diagnoses of Guantanamo detainees are made primarily to stigmatize the prisoners who caused problems for prison authorities.

According to the government's own documents,[115] born in 1981, Adnan Latif was from Ibb, Yemen. He went to high school but developed no special profession. There's no indication in the record that he was a conduct problem of any sort during his childhood or teen years. In July 1994, he sustained a skull fracture in a car accident, suffering what DoD itself described as "severe head trauma." Interestingly, it seems like an inordinate number of prominent victims of U.S. torture suffered from pre-existing head traumas, including Abu Zubaydah and Mohammed Al Qatani.

According to one of his attorneys, Marc Falkoff, the accident left him with "inner-ear problems and persistent head pain." He also lost sight in one eye. He spent much of the time between 1994-2000 "roaming from hospital to hospital and country to country, seeking inexpensive medical care."[116] The search led him to seek out a Pakistani aid worker living in Afghanistan. It was late 2001.

Latif was caught up in the U.S. invasion, captured and sent at only 19 years old to Guantanamo. In his first three years there, Latif said he was interrogated hundreds of times. When interviewed finally after three years in a Combatant Status Review Tribunal, he complained how long it had taken for Guantanamo authorities to assess his claims of innocence. Instead, Guantanamo authorities thought him "deceptive and often uncooperative." They claimed he was "a member of al-Qaida, a fighter in Usama Bin Laden's (UBL) 55th Arab Brigade, and an al-Qaida fighter in Tora Bora." Still, he was never charged with any crime.

In December 2012, U.S. Southern Command (SOUTHCOM) released a statement that Latif died from a suicidal overdose of a prescription drug, complicated by acute pneumonia.[117] The report SOUTHCOM released detailed what drugs were found in Latif's body, and provided the military's version of the events surrounding the Yemeni detainee's death.

The AR 15-6 report stated that 24 tabs of the antipsychotic drug Invega, or paliperidone, a drug similar to risperidone, were found in the dead man's stomach at the time of his death. Latif was given two tabs each day of the powerful antipsychotic (one tab of 6mg, one tab of 3mg), supposedly for agitation related to manic states of bipolar disorder.

Other drugs were found in his system as well, including another antipsychotic drug, Seroquel. Both drugs are known to cause a cardiac condition that can lead to dangerous heart arrhythmias, and even cardiac arrest, especially when combined as they were. There is no mention in the report of the possible effects of mixing and changing these drugs. Other drugs found in Latif's body included the powerfully sedating antidepressant Remeron, the antidepressant Celexa (which he was supposedly being weaned from), the tranquilizer Ativan, and various painkillers, including Percocet and codeine.

Generally, Adnan Latif was heavily medicated. The records show that in the months before his death, Latif was injected more than once with 10mg of the powerful antipsychotic drug Haldol, along with 25 mg of Benadryl to counter possible disturbing neurological and muscular side effects. According to a 2009 Department of Defense Inspector General report on the drugging of detainees, released in July 2012,[118] Haldol was routinely used as a "chemical restraint" for "uncooperative" detainees.

The AR 15-6 report explained that there was an attempt to switch Latif to monthly injections of the antipsychotic drug Invega, "administering the medication against ISN156's will," as the report put it. The plan was submitted to a "Healthcare Ethics Committee" at the Naval Medical Center in Portsmouth, Virginia. The committee approved the plan in late August 2012, but it appears the changeover to injections had not taken place before Latif died.

The report confirmed the findings of Army investigators, first reported in a Truthout article[119] by Jason Leopold, that "long-standing standard operating procedures" (SOPs) at Guantanamo were not being followed or enforced, and that such failures to follow SOP rules were implicated in Latif's death.

The final AR 15-6 report's conclusions went further than violations of SOP. It criticized differences between how SOPs are formulated between Guantanamo's medical and detention/guard commands, citing this as a cause of confusion among camp personnel. The report also cited failure to adequately train personnel, failure to hold anyone accountable for not following standard procedures, and failure to do anything about this *even when similar problems were specified in earlier reports as needing remediation.*

The lax protocols on drug administration were particularly dangerous, as drugs would at times be left out on trays attached to the cell doors. Hence, it was not observed on the day Latif died if he had taken his drugs or not. The report hinted that Latif was not the only victim of such lax methods. Unfortunately, portions of the report were heavily censored that described how Latif could have hidden drugs despite multiple guard searches. The same censorship affected portions of the report that described what happened with the so-called line-of-sight surveillance of the BHU prisoner Latif on the day he died.

The report described a health care and guard-detention regime at the Cuban-based U.S. military base that was unprofessional, sloppy, confused, and subservient to military command over healthcare practices. But even worse was the Joint Task Force – Guantanamo (JTF-GTMO) command authorities, who *failed to implement what SOUTHCOM investigators described as "many of the required changes identified in previous detainee death investigations."*

The redacted version of the report we have does not specific why "previous detainee death investigations," but it seems likely that involve the 2006 deaths, Al Hanashi, or Al Amri investigations, if not all three of them.

The failure to make such changes arguably was fatal to Adnan Latif, a traumatic brain injury victim falsely labeled a terrorist, and only years later cleared for a release that never came. Instead, it seems, the conditions of his confinement and despair over ever being released led him, like Mohamed al-Hanashi, to make numerous suicide attempts and suicidal statements, and, moreover, carried him into the far reaches of psychosis.

Poor medical practice surely played a role as well, as the report noted that an outstanding request for Latif's records for his head injury from Jordanian authorities remained unmet at the time of his death.

Latif's bizarre and obscene behaviors under the stress of incarceration were known to be too difficult for guards to long witness. "Another guard noted it was 'horrible' to be on line of sight duty for ISN156" because of behaviors considered so awful or strange they were redacted in the report.

The stress induced on Latif must have been incredible. Beyond the interrogations and the torture, the Army's report details that he was "moved from camp to camp over 67 times." In other words, his living quarters were changed on average over two times a month for ten-and-one-half years! SOUTHCOM must have felt they had to address this remarkable fact in their report, and claimed (without any supplied proof) "the moves themselves did not contribute to the detainee's death."

According to a report by another detainee, Abdelhadi Faraj (aka Abdulhadi Faraj), made to his attorney Ramzi Kassem a few months after Latif died, Latif had been moved on August 23 from the Detainee Hospital to Camp 5 – what Faraj called "the punishment camp" – returning to the detainee hospital three days later.[120]

When a day before he died Latif was told to return to Alpha Block in Camp 5, an unnamed detainee told camp authorities such a move would result in Latif committing suicide, reportedly due to bad experiences Latif associated with his previous incarceration there. According to an Al Jazeera article by Jason Leopold, Guantanamo prisoner Shaker Aamer, who occupied a cell close to Latif, told David Remes, who was an attorney for both Aamer and Latif, that "Latif had 'fought and fought' his transfer to a particular cell in Camp 5 because of the constant buzzing noise from a generator located behind a wall."[121]

Psychological reactivity to cues of past events, as well as high sensitivity to sounds (hyperacusis), is usually due to trauma, and indicative of a diagnosis of PTSD. If in fact Latif had PTSD from the events he experienced at Guantanamo – and it's generally believed a number of detainees suffer from that terrible ailment – it would be consistent with long-standing charges of abuse, as well as tortuous and cruel conditions of confinement. (It's also possible he had developed or been predisposed to PTSD from his head injury, as well.)

Instead of raising concerns about danger to the health or life of the Yemeni detainee, the report stated that Col. John V. Bogdan, the Commander of JTF-GTMO's Joint Detention Group, requested Latif be moved from the Behavioral Health Unit at the Detainee Hospital to Camp 5 for "discipline" three or four days before the Senior Medical Officer and an unnamed official (most likely either Latif's psychiatrist, psychologist, or primary care doctor) had planned a return of the beleaguered prisoner to a communal section of Camp 5.

As the report described it, on the morning of September 7, the day before he died, Latif refused to take his medications. He reportedly was quite unhappy because his portable urinal had been taken from him, because in the act of throwing it, he had supposedly splashed a guard with urine. Furthermore, this was allegedly another in a long history of such behavioral infractions.

So on the morning of September 7, Latif wrote a note to the Watch Commander that "[redacted]" (from the sense of the report his psychiatrist or another female medical official) was "'rushing him towards death' and that she was the 'cause of the problems in the detainee hospital.'" Latif asked the note be sent to Col. Bogdan. It is worth noting that this is not the first time we have heard a detainee claim a medical official was making him feel suicidal, assuming that's what Latif meant by "rushing him towards death." We have the extraordinary case of Al Hanashi some three years earlier.

The Army report does not say what the Watch Commander did with Latif's note, but that same morning, Col. Bogdan contacted an unnamed medical official (again, I surmise the psychiatrist, but it could have been a different person) and asked "whether there was a medical or psychiatric reason that would prevent ISN156 from serving his discipline time" right away, i.e., be sent back to solitary confinement in Camp 5. Seeming to bow to the pressure from a senior officer, the unnamed medical officer responded that Latif's behavioral infractions were "'very volitional behavior' and there was 'no psychiatric reason' to prevent ISN156 from serving his discipline time."

Nevertheless, there was also a "Force Protection Report," which an "analyst" brought to officials the afternoon of September 7, which stated "ISN156 was suicidal and was going to kill himself." Apparently, JTF-GTMO's Cultural Advisor got the same report and forwarded it to Bogdan "and others" in "a high-priority email." Bogdan later claimed he never saw it, but indicated to investigators that even if he had seen it, it wouldn't have made any difference in his decision to discipline Latif and send him to Camp 5.

Meanwhile, both medical and guard personnel were so worried about Latif's transfer to a solitary cell in Camp 5's Alpha Block they took special precautions to move him in such a way "so as not to alert other detainees of ISN153's pending transfer."

The SOUTHCOM investigators stood by Bogdan's decision. "In this instance, COL Bogdan acted reasonably as he had to address the frequent misconduct by ISN156. On balance, the suicidal ideation did not stand out compared to any of the other instances."

The Army report noted Latif was put in his cell under line-of-sight surveillance, which included observation via closed circuit camera. According to the report, Latif smeared food to cover the camera lens, but nothing was done about this. Two other detainees in Camp 5 were reportedly able to see right into Latif's cell, but there is no indication they were interviewed by Army investigators. The failure to even question detainee witnesses led Latif's attorney, David Remes, to label the new Army investigation "a whitewash."

According to the AR 15-6 report, confusion over how to implement the line-of-sight protocol, due to lack of training and a generally lax attitude about following SOPs with detainees, and especially with Latif, "contributed to the death of ISN156." Unremarked by mainstream press accounts thus far, the report also notes a disturbing failure to enter crucial data into the Detainee Information Management System (DIMS) the day of Latif's death, even though there is a specific SOP that governs the entry of such data during line-of-sight observation.

Of course, the failure to use DIMS for the purpose of documenting actions by detainees or actions from staff towards detainees, right at the key moment when events were leading to fatal consequences, was a key element we found in the death of Mohammed Al Hanashi three years earlier. The AR 15-6 investigation by SOUTHCOM investigators never noted that the failure to follow DIMS's SOP had any precedent in any detainee's death, which in itself is a form of cover-up.

Meanwhile, no guard was quoted in the report as saying they saw Latif take his prescribed medications. Some of the guards also thought it was strange, in retrospect, that Latif would be sleeping for 12 hours or more. In fact, he was overmedicated, either at his own hand or otherwise, and would ultimately die from the overdose.

Elsewhere in the report, investigators described an August 2012 incident, that is, only about a month before he died, when in a period of supposed agitation Latif was forcefully taken down with "emergency medication." This consisted of three shots, one each of the tranquilizer Ativan, the antipsychotic Haldol, and the sedating antihistamine Benadryl, which is applied to counter the negative side effects of the Haldol.

As noted above, and described in a DoD inspector general report, "chemical restraints" were used on detainees. It is likely that such "chemical restraints" and the "emergency medication" used on Latif are one and the same thing.

In any case, the Army report described how Latif "slept from 12 to 14 hours" after the "emergency" sequence of injections. So it is possible guards had good reason not to find it so strange that a detainee might be asleep for 12 hours or more after such chemical "discipline."

According to Faraj's account of Latif's final day (noted above), guards only went to check on Latif when another detainee, Shaker Aamer, complained that nothing had been heard from him. Faraj told his attorney about the cell where Latif died: "Adnan never left that isolation room in the punishment camp: not for exercise, food, or the restroom. He was under constant observation in that room. The door was transparent, there was a camera, and guards were watching."

The Army's report gave their version of how Latif's final "downward spiral" began, linking it to the aftermath of the June 2012 U.S. Supreme Court decision to uphold the reversal of his habeas appeal for release. U.S. officials had twice recommended Latif for release, once by an interagency national security task force in 2009, and then again in 2010 by a decision of a federal district court judge. But the right-wing judges on the D.C. Circuit Court overruled the federal district court decision, and when *Latif v. Obama* was appealed to the Supreme Court, the latter refused to take the case, leaving the Circuit Court ruling to stand, and Latif in prison now indefinitely.[122]

Latif reportedly was "furious" and "saying 'crazy stuff'" after a phone call with his attorney David Remes, who broke the terrible news to him. Yet military investigators mentioned the terrible effects of the court decision on Latif in a solitary footnote to their report. Meanwhile, medical authorities only described the depressed prisoner as "manipulative" and "willful," a behavioral management problem for the medical staff and guards.

In December 2012, an official SOUTHCOM statement concluded, "Mr. Latif died of a self-induced overdose of prescription medication. The medical examiner also concluded that acute pneumonia was a contributing factor in his death."

But in the new SOUTHCOM report, while the cause of death is specified as "paliperidone [Invega] toxicity resulting from an overdose," the autopsy is now described as saying the Armed Forces Medical Examiner "is uncertain to what extent the acute pneumonia contributed" to Latif's death. Accordingly, the report never asked or commented how Latif could be taken from the Detainee Hospital to solitary confinement in a disciplinary cell in Guantanamo's Camp 5 without anyone noticing he had "acute pneumonia."

The medical regime at Guantanamo – if it is not in fact purposely abusive – appears to reproduce the worst kinds of practices of U.S. managed care. For instance, even while the report stated the Camp 5 Officer-in-Charge told investigators she fielded "five to seven Code Yellows per week" — that is, "a potentially life-threatening medical condition requiring an immediate response" — the Detainee Hospital does not bother to staff doctors on weekends. Latif died on a Saturday.

In a final strange aside to the Army's report, it was revealed that "coincidentally" Latif's mother died on the same day as her son. The report does not state her cause of death.

The AR-15-6 report suggested that there was more to Latif's death than has been heretofore suggested by any military source. Yet in the end, the report's conclusions, its failure to seek testimony from other prisoners, and its failure to recommend any accountability measures, mar the work fatally. According to the report, written by an anonymous "objective senior officer in the rank of Colonel," a number of factors were implicated in Latif's death. Among the various factors listed in the report's Executive Summary none of them included failure to adequately search prisoners, which if Latif had in fact hoarded medications for a fatal overdosing would be something of high importance.

The Executive Summary lists the following issues Army investigators found in the Latif death:

- Guards and medical personnel "repeatedly violate" Standard Operating Procedures (SOPs)

- Guards failed to follow "line of sight" and medication SOPs, "and failed to take remedial measures after ISN156 [Latif] appeared to be sleeping an unusual amount of time." Medical personnel also violated the medication SOP

- Latif's ability to hoard medications (if we accept that is in fact what happened) was due to "inconsistent JDG [Joint Detention Group] and JMG [Joint Medical Group] SOPs" with respect to medication administration; "confusion on the part of guards, corpsmen, leadership (camp, JDG, and JMG) regarding what the SOPs require; and failure to follow medication administration SOP requirements

- Flawed training and procedures for both medical and guard personnel, and failure to document such training

- The JDG commander (Col. Bogdan), and the JMG senior leadership (presumably including its Commander, Captain Richard Stoltz and Senior Nurse Executive), seemed "largely removed from several aspects of what is going on at the tactical level" at the Behavioral Health Unit/Detainee Hospital and the camps.

- Poor communication by leadership "to ensure that their respective detainee operations practices and policies are consistent and synchronized."

- Failure of JTF-GTMO leadership to implement previous recommendations after other detainee deaths.

Later in the report, the SOUTHCOM investigator cites the various failures noted above and directly states, "These failures contributed to the death of ISN156 in that they permitted ISN156 to hoard medications" (p. 66).

The narrative around the failure to maintain the line of sight surveillance of Latif — an order that encompassed both direct (eyeball) and electronic line of sight observation — is never adequately explained in the report, seemingly because the crucial sections are highly censored. Indeed, even investigators may have been stymied in finding the truth, as the report notes how a failure by the Watch Commander "to make the line of sight entries into [camp database] DIMS as required by SOP.... did make it difficult after the fact to re-create the immediate events leading up to the point that the guards found ISN156 unresponsive."

In addition, while we are told that drugs were simply left in Latif's cell tray (or "splashbox") the day he died, supposedly he never took those drugs as he had already overdosed. But the report notes this kind of SOP violation (leaving drugs unsupervised for a detainee) may have occurred numerous times before. "Similar failures by medical staff over time, to follow the SOP may have contributed to ISN156's ability to hoard medications," the report states.

All of the above would be more than enough to throw grave doubt upon the conclusions of the report, but we also must consider the fact that other eyewitness testimony was not taken (that we know of). For instance, according to another detainee, Abdelhadi Faraj, the guards did not simply check on Latif and find him "inert." Another detainee, Shaker Aamer, called them to Latif's cell out of concern for his brother detainee's long silence.

Then there were the indications that suicidal threat was imminent. For instance, there was the internal email warning that if Latif was moved he would commit suicide, which was sent to Col. Bogdan on September 7, 2012 — the day Bogdan ordered Latif's move from the detainee hospital to a isolation punishment cell in Guantanamo's Camp 5. (A medical officer approved the move at Bogdan's request, even though, as it turned out, Latif suffered from pneumonia and never should have been moved, no matter what his psychiatric condition.)

The report stated that on September 7, "around 1400, a [one word redaction] analyst from the [four or five word redaction — possibly Behavioral Science Consultation Team?] arrived with a Force Protection Report indicating [one word redaction] was saying that ISN156 was suicidal and was going to kill himself. [One or two word redaction] recalled asking the analyst whether he knew what method ISN156 intended to use to kill himself. The analyst indicated that he did not know and followed up the exchange with an email."

A footnote in the report claimed it was this very warning that prompted the order to place Latif on both direct and electronic line-of-sight surveillance.

The report continued (p. 20 – and I must beg the reader's patience, as the government redactions make this section a dense read): "the JTF-GTMO Cultural Advisor ([three or four words redacted]) also received the same Force Protection Report, in a high priority email at 1430 on 7 September 2012. [One or two words redacted] forwarded the email to COL Bogdan, [two or three words redacted] (the Deputy JDG Commander), and others in a high priority email, adding that 'pushing 156 to the corner never works to our advantage.' COL Bogdan indicated he was not aware of the email until sometime the following day, Saturday."

Elsewhere in the report, returning again to the 7 September "high-priority" email, it was observed: "Although COL Bodgan did not receive the email until the following day, he stated that it would not have affected his decision to transfer ISN156 to Camp 5, because ISN156 was known to make 'melodramatic' statements. In this instance, COL Bogdan acted reasonably as he had to address the frequent misconduct by ISN156. On balance, the suicidal ideation did not stand out compared to any of the other instances" (p. 64).

But SOUTHCOM's own report, which quotes warnings from medical personnel, suggested otherwise! Indeed, just how often were "high-priority emails" sent to COL Bogdan or his predecessors warning of a detainee's suicide? It's also worth noting that other news reports describe Latif as saying camp authorities were pushing him "towards death every moment."

Latif also complained to his attorney David Remes that guards were leaving contraband in his cell by which he could hurt himself. As noted in the previous chapter, in a May 25, 2010 letter to Remes and another attorney, Marc Falcoff, Latif complained that rather than provide him with items he needed, like soap and eyeglasses, camp authorities gave him items, such as scissors, with which he could hurt himself. I have heard that other detainees have made such accusations of placement in their cells of articles to use for self-harm. To my knowledge, no investigation into such charges has ever taken place.

In the same letter to his attorneys, Latif seemed to predict his own death:

"Here I am in the big hospital of the camp where death is certain. They insist, while I am in this condition, on looking at my private parts and then letting me urinate and defecate in my bed while my hands and legs are bound. I am not allowed to go to the bathroom and not allowed to pray. So, no need for courts or justice. Real justice for me is to die instead of being tortured. All what happened and what I have mentioned is in their daily reports and their computers. After the surgery [to remove coins he swallowed, or, as he maintained, camp personnel "made me swallow"], they stopped feeding me or letting me eat by orders from the surgeon.

"It seems that I might have to send you my body parts and flesh to make you believe me and to believe to what degree of misery I have reached. I am happy to die just to get away from a non-extinguishable fire and no-end torture.

"Marc and David: In the end, I am a human being."

Chapter 7
Concluding Thoughts

In March 2012, Christof Heyns, the UN Special Rapporteur on extrajudicial, summary or arbitrary executions, responded to an inquiry by this reporter regarding the information on the deaths of Abdul Rahman Al Amri and Mohammad Salih Al Hanashi gleaned from the autopsies I'd discovered. The analysis of the autopsies had previously been published at the website Truthout.[123]

Heynes wrote, "We are looking into this matter, and I have received provisional feedback, thank you for bringing it to my attention."[124]

After receiving Heynes feedback, I asked the Department of Defense if they had been in contact with Heyns' office on this issue, or had any other comment on the earlier Truthout article about the two Guantanamo detainee deaths. DoD Spokesman Lt. Col. Todd Breasseale told me, "Our ongoing relationships with the various concerned offices of the United Nations are positive, open, and constructive."

"JTF Guantanamo conducts safe, humane, legal and transparent care and custody of detainees, including those convicted by military commission and those ordered released by a court. We continually evaluate these procedures to ensure that the care, safety, and security of all concerned at the JTF is a top priority," Breasseale said.

Yet, so far as I know, nothing ever came from this UN referral. I never heard more from Mr. Heynes, and the matter of the detainee suicides has faded from the public view, which raises an important question: why bother to continue to investigate or press for accountability in regards to these deaths? The Barack Obama administration continues to release prisoners from Guantanamo, and only some four dozen or so remain in the prison as of this writing.

Torture is considered a crime against humanity. As far back as the European Enlightenment, the philosopher Voltaire reminded us that of the laws most important to human liberation, the first concern universal tolerance, the second concern the abolition against torture.

The Guantanamo detainees were held in total thrall to the greatest power on this earth. Such power had the highest responsibility to treat the powerless in their possession with humanity and respect; instead they treated them with contempt, objects for experimental manipulation and sadistic torture, and ultimately political pawns to advance military and political careers and agendas.

The Heynes referral was followed by the publication of Joe Hickman's investigation into the 2006 deaths of three Guantanamo detainees, which while it had significant press interest, failed to induce further government response or even a general call for further investigation or accountability by the public at large. This is very disappointing, and I believe future generations will be hard pressed to understand or forgive the societal failure to hold accountable those who engaged in torture, or refused to prosecute it.

Sadly, U.S. use of torture did not end, as is popularly believed, with the issuance of the January 2009 order, "Ensuring Lawful Interrogations," by then new President Barack Obama. Stories about torture by U.S. authorities continued.[125] Rendition of prisoners remained U.S. policy, and torture by U.S. government proxies was reported again and again.[126]

Obama's 2009 Executive Order promised that all U.S. national security interrogations would adhere to the standards of the Army's Field Manual on interrogations, FM 2-22.3, which were supposed to be free from use of torture. But at the close of 2014, a UN committee that periodically meets to assess country compliance with the UN's Convention Against Torture treaty, to which the U.S. is a signatory, found the Army Field Manual contained a section, known as Appendix M, that used techniques, including isolation, sleep deprivation and sensory deprivation, that amounted to "ill treatment" and raised concern over torture. Indeed, one portion of Appendix M, known as "field expedient separation," allowed the use of a type of sensory deprivation that could "create a state of psychosis with the detainee."[127]

Recently, there has been a spate of articles giving further details about Appendix M, how and when it has been used under the Obama administration, and what is wrong with it.[128] The recent interest has been encouraging.

What conclusions have I drawn about the manner of death in the cases explored in this book?

Al Amri was discovered hanging in his cell. His hands had been loosely tied behind his back. I have criticized the Department of Defense for not following forensic SOP and considering homicide as a possibility in his death. I have raised the possibility that Al Amri died in much the same way the 2006 detainees did, by asphyxiation via a rag thrust down his throat. We must await the declassification of a good deal more material to see if my hypothesis bears further investigation, resting, as it does on the missing piece of cloth that was apparently thrown out with the medical trash (unless it disappeared in some other fashion.)

A military cover-up of prisoner or detainee murder is not sadly a totally strange or "out there" concept. In 2005, the online medical journal, Medscape General Medicine published a study of cases in which prisoners held by U.S. defense forces "potentially died because of mistreatment or under suspicious circumstances."[129] Dr. Steven H. Miles, professor of medicine and bioethics at the University of Minnesota, wrote the article, which looked at "reports of U.S. Army and U.S. Navy criminal investigations, death certificates, autopsy reports, sworn statements, official correspondence between military personnel, and U.S. Department of Defense policies."

Miles pointed out there were practical difficulties related to the military's investigations. The Armed Forces Office of the Medical Examiner (AFME) had budget cutbacks in 2002, not long after Guantanamo opened, which "left the AFME with only 2 forensic pathologists; in 2004, it had 13," Miles wrote. He went on: "The AFME was not prepared to investigate the deaths of prisoners who may have died of torture. Its pathologists have published little on forensic pathology and are not known to have specialized expertise in investigating or documenting the injuries of persons who died under torture.

Miles complained that examiners didn't make "any inquiry into the nature of... interrogation or confinement" of a prisoner. Forensic medical evidence was mishandled. Meanwhile, the U.S. Department of Defense "has failed to allow an independent review of autopsy photographs, particularly of the exterior of the bodies, which may show trauma that went unnoted." Indeed, no autopsy photos of any of the deceased detainees have ever been released. Meanwhile, other medical authorities have described how "some medical personnel neglected detainees' medical needs and collaborated with coercive interrogations."[130] In other words, there's plenty to be suspicious about in relation to the government's narrative and documents. But the U.S. press in general (with a few notable exceptions) has accepted government accounts of all the deaths at Guantanamo.

In Al Hanashi's death, a more solid case of suicide seems to be evident, given the intense spate of suicidal behavior the deeply depressed prisoner demonstrated. But there are a number of discrepancies in his case that makes this more than a tragic case of self-destruction. Such discrepancies or mysteries include: Al Hanashi's ligature was said at one point to be twisted on the right side of his neck, another time on the left side; the "elastic band" from his "brief" (supposedly used to kill himself) does not match the type of underwear in use at Guantanamo at this time; the timeline leaves unexplained why he was not on suicide watch after multiple recent attempts, or why there was a large gap in time that he was not observed, contrary to SOP procedures.

Indeed, how did Al Hanashi, or any of the other detainees find the time and space to create a ligature or rope, to hide medications or razors? According to the Camp Delta SOP, cells are searched "whenever a detainee exits a cell or prior to his return to his cell.... A minimum of three random cell searches will be done on day shift and swing shift."

Showers and recreation areas are searched "before and after every detainee use.... When searching," the operating manual explains, "use a systematic method to ensure all areas are covered." Midnight shift has the special duty of conducting a "visual search of the cells and detainees every ten minutes by walking through the block." "All unusual activity" is to be reported. In general, all detainees are searched "at a minimum of each time they are removed from a cell."

For detainees involved in Self Harm or Injured Behavior, there is a Self Harm/Injured Behavior SOP that requires that "viewing doors will remain open at all times."

"Each prisoner has an assigned suicide prevention blanket, and personnel are on the alert for self-harm behaviors."[131]

Finally, there were the evident attempts to stop and at times hide or destroy evidence of what exactly happened around the time of Al Hanashi's death. The shutdown of Guantanamo's computer system, possibly ordered by NCIS or some other military, law enforcement or intelligence official, and that later disappearance of two days of computer logs from the time of his death, raises suspicions that more was happening than simple, if tragic, suicide.

The discrepancies surrounding Al Hanashi's death have led me to believe the most likely cause of his death was facilitated suicide, which itself is a kind of murder. All the available data now argues that camp guards and/or prison health officials, with or without the connivance of camp leadership, very likely provided the very mentally ill Al Hanashi with the means and the available time to kill himself.

That leaves the issue of motive. Besides some unknown political reason, or the effect of experiments or drugs on the prisoner, I believe it's possible that prison hospital officials and/or guards had simply tired of Al Hanashi's chronic suicidality and self-mutilation (he had been consistently banging his head on the prison camps walls), and decided to let him die (criminal neglect) or facilitated his death by the proffer of materials and opportunity to make the fatal attempt. This also seems a possibility in the death of Adnan Latif, as well. The fact

Al Hanashi was seen as a leader of other detainees raises the possibility that he was also killed or allowed to die as a message to other detainees, or to demoralize others by the death of one of their leaders.

I cannot rule out, either, that his death was related to some of the experimentation that went on at Guantanamo, or was related to knowledge the prisoner had that the government wanted silenced.

If there was facilitated suicide, which in effect amounts to murder, it is not unprecedented. Indeed, an article from 2009 describes just such a prison "suicide," allegedly arranged by prison personnel in the case of Matthew Bullock, a mentally ill prisoner at the State Correctional Institution at Dallas, Texas.[132]

According to an article in the Wilkes-Barre Times Leader,[133] "Bret Grote, an investigator with the Fed Up! Chapter of the Human Rights Coalition, said prisoners who were confined in cells near Bullock contacted the organization claiming that Bullock, though a known suicide risk, had been moved from a video-equipped cell to one without monitoring capabilities.

"On the morning of the suicide, two guards at the Jackson Township facility had been kicking on Bullock's cell door, saying, 'Kill yourself, you little p****,' according to one prisoner report, Grote said."

According to the article, prisoners at the Dallas prison said staff there wouldn't put Bullock on suicide watch, despite his stated intention to kill himself. It wasn't long after stating such intentions that Bullock was found "hanging dead from his cell door...."

Did something like this happen to Al Hanashi? Were pills sufficient to commit suicide essentially given to Latif so he could harm himself, the way he claimed guards gave him scissors?

According to one online description, "facilitated suicide" "occurs because of clinician indifference."[134] But as in the case of Bullock and most likely Al Hanashi, and possibly

Latif, the actions can be even more active than the mere withdrawal of necessary care.

Former detainee Binyam Mohamed made the important point that if any of these prisoners indeed had been driven to kill themselves, they did so under the auspices of a torture regime. Hence, it was still the presence of abuse and torture, and indefinite detention, what Guantanamo authorities themselves called "conditions of confinement," that was responsible for the deaths of these prisoners.

We must pause for a moment to consider just what Guantanamo was really about. Was it an intelligence center for interrogation? Was it heavily involved in the recruitment of double agents to return to the field of battle, so to speak, in the "war on terror"? Or was it primarily a large experimental facility, testing numerous kinds of procedures on the multi-ethnic detainee population?

The weight fluctuations of the detainees, as detailed in the chapters above, calls to mind the fact that the interrogators at Guantanamo were taught a version of a chart in coercive methods of interrogation that was drawn up by a government researcher almost sixty years ago. The fact was revealed in the 2008 Senate Armed Services Committee investigation into detainee abuse.[135]

The chart, created by sociologist Albert Biderman in the later 1950s, mentions various ways used to break down prisoners to do the bidding of interrogators or government authorities. The general methods include use of isolation, monopolization of perception, induced debilitation or exhaustion, use of threats, occasional indulgences, demonstration of "omnipotence" and "omniscience," degradation, and enforcement of trivial demands. Under "induced exhaustion," Biderman mentions the use of "semi-starvation."

One of the researchers who met with CIA researchers and CIA-linked psychologists, physicians and scientists, and who was a contemporary of Biderman's, was Dr. Josef Brozek of the famous Minnesota Starvation Study. At a symposium of the Group for the Advancement of Psychiatry in 1956, Brozek told other researchers, who were discussing "Factors Used to Increase the Susceptibility of Individuals to Forceful Indoctrination," about the use of semi-starvation in breaking down prisoners.

"A situation in which food would be offered on certain occasions and would be withdrawn on other occasions would constitute a more intensive psychological stress than food restriction alone," Dr. Brozek wrote. "It would result in severe frustration, and would more readily break a man's moral fiber. By combining such a treatment with other forms of deprivation and insult, one could expect eventually to induce a "breakdown" in the majority of human beings."[136]

Some decades later, were the weight fluctuations of detainees solely due to hunger striking and forced feeding, as awful as the latter may be? Or were there other, more grisly investigations being done?

The strange use of antimalarial drugs on detainees, especially mefloquine, such that their presence were sought in toxicology reports done on at least four of the supposed Guantanamo suicides, also seems to argue for some kind of experimentation taking place.

The very use of Behavioral Science Consultation Teams, staffed at various times by psychologists and psychiatrists, who studied the effects of behavioral interventions at Guantanamo, appear to be involved in some kind of research on the effects of imprisonment conditions.

Finally, there was the recent revelation that the CIA's contracts with former military psychologists James Mitchell and Bruce Jessen involved first and foremost the use of research on prisoners. The contracts for James Mitchell, for instance, state that he is supposed to provide the CIA's interrogation program with work on CIA "applied research efforts" and "conduct specified, time-limited research projects," while "applying research methodology to meet OTS [redacted] goals and objectives." [137]

OTS is the CIA's Office of Technical Services, and was involved in the creation and vetting of the CIA's torture program. OTS was also the section of the CIA that was involved in running the controversial experimentation program MKULTRA in from the 1950s and 1960s. It is only reasonable to assume that the Department of Defense torture program also involved research, if it actually wasn't linked up to the CIA program as part of a highly classified Special Access Program.

The deaths of the Guantanamo detainees call out for an independent investigation. But it's unlikely anything approaching that will occur. One reason rarely mentioned is the indifference of the American public to the crimes that took place and still take place at the US gulag-style prison. A signal cause for such indifference is the subordination of American liberalism to the electoral needs of presidential politics. With the looming 2016 presidential election between Hillary Clinton and Donald Trump, the fate of those in a prison where Obama has put his stamp of approval over the indefinite detention of the prisoners – even if he has towards the end of his administration finally escalated the transfer of prisoners out of Guantanamo – is a matter of little account to those who see in the election of a Democratic president the overarching goal of their political lives.

Additionally, Obama has infamously told his followers that they must "not look back" at the crimes that took place under the Bush administration, and that includes the torture of "war on terror" prisoners. But Al Hanashi and Latif both died on Obama's watch. It's not about a failure of accountability over the past any more, but about burying a moral imperative against torture and murder so your candidate or their political party can be elected.

The failure to fully investigate the deaths of Al Amri, Al Hanashi, Latif, and the fate of the other Guantanamo detainees, including the last Guantanamo "suicide", Inayatullah (aka Hajji Nassim), indicts America and its defenders. When those who are held under the full weight and power of the U.S. government cannot be adequately protected and treated humanely, when there is no accountability for crimes committed against prisoners and detainees, against the helpless and bound, then all the grand statements about democracy and justice are revealed to be a sham.

Acknowledgments

Any work of this sort rests upon the labors of many others who have labored to get out the truth about what happened, and what arguably still goes on in regards to U.S. torture and rendition. I am especially appreciative of the work of the ACLU in obtaining and releasing relevant documents. Wikileaks, through their release of "The Guantanamo Files," was also instrumental in furthering our understanding of how the detainees were perceived, and I would add, manipulated, by interrogators at Guantanamo. The attorneys for the detainees have worked assiduously to represent their clients under the most difficult conditions, and have been able at times to get the actual words of the detainees out to the public. As noted in the book, some of the detainees themselves, after release from Guantanamo, in conditions that require tremendous emotional courage, wrote about their experiences in the U.S. torture prisons, and their contribution has been invaluable.

I want to thank the following individuals for their assistance at various times in my research and writing on torture over the years, though not necessarily regarding the specific content of this book. So thanks to: Jason Leopold (who encouraged me in so many ways, and who by example showed me what good reporting is), Sheila Meneely (for her patience, support, comments, and proofreading), Joe Hickman (who pioneered the way), Mark Denbeaux and his student assistants at Seton Hall University School of Law's Center for Policy and Research (for perspicacity and integrity), Almerindo Ojeda (for dedication, documentation, and insight), David Remes (for caring and struggling against tremendous odds), Andy Worthington (for seeing and acting on what was important), Kevin Gosztola, Marcy Wheeler, Remington Nevin (who grounded the mefloquine discussion in medical science), Michael S. Kearns (who taught us more about SERE), Douglas Valentine (for his ground-breaking work), Alyosia Brooks, Rupert Stone, Mark Fallon, Jane Hamsher, Uwe Jacobs, and Ky Henderson (who read an early draft of one of the book's chapters). I also want to thank Christina Cusack at the NCIS FOIA office, and Marco Villalobos and Samuel London at SOUTHCOM's FOIA office. Whatever my frustrations with their departments, I am aware these individuals labor under the pressure of immense bureaucracies, and with insufficient budgets to complete their tasks. My apologies if I left anyone out. Listing the names above does not constitute an endorsement of this book or my work in general by any of these individuals. The opinions expressed throughout are mine alone, and not to be attributed necessarily to anyone else, unless they are so quoted.

About the Author

Jeffrey S. Kaye is a psychologist with a long-time private practice in San Francisco, California. He has written on topics concerning U.S. policy on torture and on political topics in general for online publications, including Alternet, The Guardian, Firedoglake/The Dissenter/Shadowproof, Al Jazeera America, Truthout, and The Public Record. He has his own blog, Invictus, at http://valtinsblog.blogspot.com, where he writes under the screen name "Valtin."

In 2007, at the American Psychological Association convention in San Francisco, he spoke about the history of psychological research into sensory deprivation, and its utilization by the U.S. government for purposes of interrogation and torture. The presentation was drawn from a larger historical essay, "Isolation, Sensory Deprivation, and Sensory Overload: History, Research, and Interrogation Policy, from the 1950s to the Present Day," published in the National Lawyers Guild's publication, Guild Practitioner.[138] Dr. Kaye's research utilizing the Freedom of Information Act led to the 2014 declassification of a less redacted version of the CIA's classic KUBARK interrogation/torture manual.[139]

Endnotes

[1] Translation from Koran at Ali 'Imran (Family of Imran), URL: http://quran.com/3/185

[2] See URL: http://www.buddytv.com/articles/ncis/best-ncis-quotes-from-charade-59502.aspx (accessed June 12, 2016)

[3] Ave Mince-Didier, "The Circumstantial Evidence Jury Instruction," Nolo, URL: http://www.criminaldefenselawyer.com/resources/the-circumstantial-evidence-jury-instruction.htm

[4] Guantanamo 2004 SOP, Section 6-15 (a), as referenced in Mark Denbeaux et al., Death in Camp Delta, Seton Hall University School of Law, Center for Policy and Research, December 7, 2009, p. 51, URL: http://law.shu.edu/ProgramsCenters/PublicIntGovServ/policyresearch/upload/gtmo_death_camp_delta.pdf

[5] "Suicides" is in quotes because there are some real questions as to whether the deaths of three detainees in June 2006 were indeed by suicide. Their deaths were studied in detail by a former guard present the night the deaths occurred. The guard, Joseph Hickman, wrote up his findings in his 2015 book, Murder in Camp Delta: A Staff Sergeant's Pursuit of the Truth About Guantanamo Bay, Simon and Schuster. The verdict of suicide in the 2006 deaths was also challenged in an award winning article by Scott Horton at Harper's, "The Guantánamo 'Suicides': A Camp Delta sergeant blows the whistle," Harper's Magazine, March 2010, URL: http://harpers.org/archive/2010/03/the-guantanamo-suicides/; and in a report by Seton Hall University School of Law, Center for Policy and Research, Death in Camp Delta, December 7, 2009, URL: http://law.shu.edu/ProgramsCenters/PublicIntGovServ/policyresearch/upload/gtmo_death_camp_delta.pdf

[6] June 4, 2009 "Statement" of the Chief of Behavioral Health Services for JTF GTMO. See Al Hanashi documents, Part 8, pp. 16-18, URL: http://GuantanamoTruth.com

[7] June 4, 2009, Guard statement. See Al Hanashi documents, Part 9, pg. 12, URL: http://GuantanamoTruth.com

[8] "A conversation this side of the wire: Transcription," UC Davis Center for the Study of Human Rights in the Americas, April 30, 2010, URL: http://humanrights.ucdavis.edu/events/a-conversation-this-side-of-the-wire-transcription

[9] Jeffrey Kaye, "Murder at Guantanamo?" Truthout, November 20, 2009, URL: http://www.truth-out.org/archive/component/k2/item/86847:murder-at-guantanamo

[10] Naomi Wolf, "What Happened to Mohamed al Hanashi?" Project Syndicate, August 31, 2009, URL: https://www.project-syndicate.org/commentary/what-happened-to-mohamed-al-hanashi

[11] R. K. Sharma, Concise Textbook of Forensic Medicine and Toxicology, Elsevier India, 2007, p. 55

[12] U.S. Army, "Enclosures to Schmidt-Furlow Report: AR 15-6 Investigation into FBI Allegations of Detainee Abuse at Guantanamo Bay Detention Facility," June 9, 2005, URL: http://hrlibrary.umn.edu/OathBetrayed/Schmidt-Furlow%20Report%20Enclosures%20II.pdf

[13] Feroz Abbassi, Rhuhel Ahmed, Moazzam Begg, Richard Belmar, Tarek Dergoul, Jamal al-Harith, Asif Iqbal, Martin Mubanga and Shafiq Rasul, "Former Guantanamo Britons: Statement on the Deaths in Guantánamo Bay," Cageprisoners, June 13, 2006, URL: http://old.cageprisoners.com/articles.php?id=14510

[14] See http://www.dod.mil/pubs/foi/Reading_Room/Detainee_Related/DicksteinGTMO_SJA_DeathInvestigation.pdf, pg. SJA-3. The "SJA" in the link above refers to the Staff Judge Advocate's office, which conducted its own investigation into the 2006 suicides.

[15] Lt. (ret.) Richard Lichten, "Jail Suicides, Attempted and Completed: Avoiding Allegations of Deliberate Indifference," Police and Jail Procedures, Inc., undated, URL: http://www.policeandjailprocedures.com/live/jail-suicides,-attempted-and-completed-avoiding-allegations-of-deliberate-indifference.html

[16] David Hicks, Guantanamo, My Journey, Random House, 2012, p. 356.

[17] Jeffrey Kaye, "A Guantanamo Connection? Documents Show CIA Stockpiled Antimalaria Drugs as 'Incapacitating Agents'", Truthout, June 6, 2012, URL: http://www.truth-out.org/news/item/9601-a-guantanamo-connection-documents-show-cia-stockpiled-antimalaria-drugs-as-incapacitating-agents

[18] While not referencing any particular detainee on the mefloquine issue, a 2013 report by the Institute on Medicine as a Profession (IMAP) and the Open Society Foundations (OSF) noted the following: "Questions have arisen about the unexplained administration of an antimalaria drug with neuropsychiatric side effects to detainees at Guantánamo, including whether there were intelligence or security reasons rather than medical reasons for doing so. As the conduct of a member of the task Force has been questioned on this subject, the task Force does not address the matter here, but urges that the circumstances of the use of mefloquine, including the reasons for choosing it, be addressed as part of the full investigation of medical practices we recommend." See Ethics Abandoned: Medical Professionalism and Detainee Abuse in the "War on Terror," [p. 48], URL: http://hrp.law.harvard.edu/wp-content/uploads/2013/11/IMAP-EthicsTextFinal2.pdf

[19] Joseph Hickman, Chapter 25, "The Mefloquine Motive," Murder in Camp Delta: A Staff Sergeant's Pursuit of the Truth About Guantanamo Bay, Simon and Schuster, 2015.

[20] David H. Hoffman, et al., Report to the Special Committee of the Board of Directors of the American Psychological Association: Independent Review Relating to APA Ethics Guidelines, National Security Interrogations, and Torture, Sidley Austin LLP, September 4, 2015, URL: http://www.apa.org/independent-review/revised-report.pdf

In my opinion, Hoffman's report, though containing worthwhile material, is unavoidably compromised by conflicts of interest by both Hoffman himself and by his law firm, Sidley Austin. I explored these issues in two articles online: Jeffrey Kaye, "APA 'Independent' Torture Review Led by Attorney Who Worked With CIA's Tenet," Shadowproof, December 7, 2014, URL: https://shadowproof.com/2014/12/07/apa-independent-torture-review-led-by-attorney-who-worked-with-cias-tenet/, and "New Questions About Conflict-of-Interest Throw Doubt on APA's 'Independent Review' of CIA Links," Shadowproof, June 3, 2015, URL: https://shadowproof.com/2015/06/03/new-questions-about-conflict-of-interest-throw-doubt-on-apas-independent-investigation-on-cia-links/

[21] Valtin (aka Jeffrey Kaye), "DHS Behavioral Research Group proposed 'use of Guantanamo Bay subjects as data'", Invictus, June 22, 2016, URL: http://valtinsblog.blogspot.com/2016/06/dhs-behavioral-research-group-proposed.html

[22] "Kabrin, Mike" to "Scott Gerwehr," Email dated December 7, 2004, URL: http://www.hoffmanreportapa.com/resources/memofromNRtoJR_Redacted.pdf (accessed August 28, 2016)

[23] "Denial and Deception," Wikipedia, URL: https://en.wikipedia.org/wiki/Denial_and_deception

[24] Jason Leopold, "The CIA Paid This Contractor $40 Million to Review Torture Documents," Vice News, July 27, 2015, URL: https://news.vice.com/article/the-cia-paid-this-contractor-40-million-to-review-torture-documents (accessed August 28, 2016)

[25] See, for instance, Scott Allen, Nathaniel Raymond, Experiments in Torture: Evidence of Human Subject Research and Experimentation in the "Enhanced" Interrogation Program, Physicians for Human Rights, June 2010, URL: https://s3.amazonaws.com/PHR_Reports/Experiments_in_Torture.pdf; and Mark P. Denbeaux, Jonathan Hafetz, Joshua Denbeaux, et al., Guantanamo: America's Battle Lab, Seton Hall University School of Law, Center for Policy and Research, Jan. 2015, URL: https://law.shu.edu/policy-

research/upload/guantanamo-americas-battle-lab-january-2015.pdf; also Jeffrey Kaye, "US Government Classifies Term 'America's Battle Lab' in War on Terror' in Pentagon Report," Shadowproof, March 15, 2015, URL: https://shadowproof.com/2015/03/15/us-government-classifies-term-battle-lab-in-war-on-terror-in-pentagon-report/ (accessed June 26 , 2016)

[26] See Andy Worthington, "The Afghan Hero Who Died in Guantánamo," Huffington Post, March 8, 2008, URL: http://www.huffingtonpost.com/andy-worthington/the-afghan-hero-who-died-_b_90518.html (accessed July 17, 2016)

[27] Minutes, Armed Forces Epidemiological Board Meeting, February 19, 2002, URL: http://web.archive.org/web/20120306053751/http://www.health.mil/dhb/afeb/meeting/Transcripts/Day1Transcripts.pdf (accessed July 4, 2016).

See also: Jeffrey Kaye, "Unreported Detainee Deaths at Guantanamo in Jan-Feb 2002?," Invictus, December 19, 2010, URL: http://valtinsblog.blogspot.com/2010/12/unreported-detainee-deaths-at_19.html

[28] Jason Leopold and Jeffrey Kaye, "Ex-Guantanamo Official Was Told Not to Discuss Policy Surrounding Antimalarial Drug Used on Detainees," Truthout, December 20, 2010, URL: http://www.truth-out.org/news/item/254:exguantanamo-official-was-told-not-to-discuss-policy-surrounding-antimalarial-drug-used-on-detainees (accessed July 4, 2016)

[29] Mark Denbeaux et al., Death in Camp Delta, Seton Hall University School of Law, Center for Policy and Research, December 7, 2009, URL: http://law.shu.edu/ProgramsCenters/PublicIntGovServ/policyresearch/upload/gtmo_death_camp_delta.pdf

[30] See URL: http://www.nytimes.com/interactive/2014/12/09/world/cia-torture-report-document.html?_r=0

[31] Mark Danner, "The Red Cross Torture Report, What It Means," New York Review of Books, April 30, 2009, URL:

http://www.nybooks.com/articles/2009/04/30/the-red-cross-torture-report-what-it-means/

[32] Murat Kurnaz, Five Years of My Life: An Innocent Man in Guantanamo, St. Martin's Press, 2009 (reprint edition)

[33] Moazzam Begg and Victoria Brittain, Enemy Combatant: My Imprisonment at Guantanamo, Bagram, And Kandahar, The New Press, 2006.

[34] Mamdouh Habib with Julia Collingwood, My Story: The Tale of a Terrorist Who Wasn't, Scribe Publications Pty Ltd., 2009.

[35] Mohamedou Ould Slahi, Guantanamo Diary (ed. Larry Siems), Little Brown and Company, 2015.

[36] Fault Lines, "The dark prisoners: Inside the CIA's torture programme," Al Jazeera, March 27, 2016, URL: http://www.aljazeera.com/indepth/features/2016/03/dark-prisoners-cia-torture-programme-160326051331796.html

[37] Jason Leopold, "EXCLUSIVE: David Hicks: One of Guantanamo Bay's First Detainees Breaks His Silence," Truthout, February 15, 2011, URL: http://www.truth-out.org/news/item/258:exclusive-one-of-guantanamo-bays-first-detainees-breaks-his-silence

[38] UN Commission on Human Rights, Situation of Detainees at Guantánamo Bay, 27 February 2006, E/CN.4/2006/120, p. 21, URL: http://www.refworld.org/docid/45377b0b0.html [accessed 12 June 2016]

[39] Available at URL: https://www.amnesty.ie/sites/default/files/report/2010/04/guantanamo%20conditions%20main%20text-FINAL.pdf

[40] Jim Risen and Tim Golden, "3 Prisoners Commit Suicide at Guantánamo," New York Times, June 10, 2006, URL: http://www.nytimes.com/2006/06/11/us/11gitmo.html

[41] Scott Horton, "The Guantánamo 'Suicides': A Camp Delta sergeant blows the whistle," Harper's Magazine, March 2010, URL: http://harpers.org/archive/2010/03/the-guantanamo-suicides/

[42] Seton Hall University School of Law, Center for Policy and Research, Death in Camp Delta, December 7, 2009, URL: http://law.shu.edu/ProgramsCenters/PublicIntGovServ/policyresearch/upload/gtmo_death_camp_delta.pdf

[43] Almerindo Ojeda, "Death in Guantanamo: Suicide or Dryboarding?" Truthout, November 3, 2011, URL: http://www.truth-out.org/news/item/4511:death-in-guantanamo-suicide-or-dryboarding (accessed June 12, 2016)

[44] Andy Worthington, "Remembering a Death at Guantánamo, Six Years Since I Began Writing About the Prison as an Independent Journalist," June 2, 2013, URL: http://www.andyworthington.co.uk/2013/06/02/remembering-a-death-at-guantanamo-six-years-since-i-began-writing-about-the-prison-as-an-independent-journalist/

[45] UN Committee Against Torture, "Concluding observations on the third to fifth periodic reports of United States of America," November 20, 2014, URL: http://tbinternet.ohchr.org/Treaties/CAT/Shared%20Documents/USA/INT_CAT_COC_USA_18893_E.pdf

[46] Jeffrey Kaye, "Contrary to Obama's promises, the US military still permits torture," The Guardian, January 25, 2014, URL: http://www.theguardian.com/commentisfree/2014/jan/25/obama-administration-military-torture-army-field-manual

[47] Jeffrey Kaye, "Deconstructing the Campaign to Malign Award-Winning Article on Guantanamo 'Suicides'," Truthout, June 1, 2011, URL: http://www.truth-out.org/news/item/1381:deconstructing-the-campaign-to-malign-awardwinning-article-on-guantanamo-suicides

[48] Jason Leopold, "How Guantanamo Became America's Interrogation 'Battle Lab'", January 12, 2015, Vice News, URL: https://news.vice.com/article/how-guantanamo-became-americas-interrogation-battle-lab

[49] This army investigation, known as an AR 15-6 report, can be accessed at URL: https://www.box.com/s/enhc8gdv9z1tw80xvwho

[50] Kathleen T. Rhem, "Automated System Helps Guantanamo Guards Track Detainees," February 17, 2005, American Forces Press Service, URL: http://archive.defense.gov/news/newsarticle.aspx?id=25866 (accessed September 11, 2016)

[51] See Army's AR 15-6 report on death of 2006 detainees at http://www.dod.mil/pubs/foi/Reading_Room/Detainee_Related/DicksteinGTMO_SJA_DeathInvestigation.pdf (accessed August 24, 2016)

[52] See URL: http://www.dod.mil/pubs/foi/Reading_Room/Detainee_Related/DicksteinGTMO_SJA_DeathInvestigation2.pdf, p. SJA 237 (accessed August 24, 2016)

[53] The Seton Hall School of Law researchers at the Center for Policy and Research spent some time analyzing the contradictions in the various DoD investigations into the 2006 "suicides" in their February 2012 report, "DOD Contradicts DOD: An Analysis of the Response to *Death in Camp Delta*," URL: http://law.shu.edu/ProgramsCenters/PublicIntGovServ/policyresearch/upload/dod_contradicts_dod_final2410.pdf (accessed August 31, 2016)

[54] See URL: http://www.dod.mil/pubs/foi/Reading_Room/Detainee_Related/DicksteinGTMO_SJA_DeathInvestigation.pdf pp. SJA 37-39, SJA 83

[55] This information comes from a memorandum dated "10 June 2008" to the "Commander, United States Southern Command, 3511 NW 9lst Avenue, Miami, FL 33172," titled "SUBJECT: Recommendation for Continued Detention Under DoD Control (CD) for Guantanamo Detainee, ISN US9YM-000078DP (S)." The memo was one of many released as part of Wikileaks Guantanamo Files, URL: https://wikileaks.org/gitmo/prisoner/78.html

[56] One can access a copy of Hanashi's autopsy report, reproduced as part of The Guantanamo Testimonials Project at the Center for the Study of Human Rights in the Americas

(CSHRA) at University of California, Davis, URL: http://humanrights.ucdavis.edu/projects/the-guantanamo-testimonials-project/testimonies/prisoner-testimonies/autopsy_muhammad_al_hanashi.pdf.

Researchers and the public at large owe a large debt of gratitude to CSHRA's director, Professor Almerindo Ojeda. Ojeda wrote an important article on the possibility that the torture technique "dryboarding" was involved in the 2006 deaths of three Guantanamo detainees, which the Department of Defense pronounced were suicides. See Almerindo Ojeda, "Death in Guantanamo: Suicide or Dryboarding?" November 3, 2011, Truthout, URL: http://www.truth-out.org/news/item/4511:death-in-guantanamo-suicide-or-dryboarding

[57] See URL: https://commons.wikimedia.org/w/index.php?title=File:ISN_78_--_Mohammad_Ahmed_Abdullah_Saleh_Al_Hanashi%27s_--_Guantanamo_weights.jpg&redirect=no Note: The accuracy of the weights given, unfortunately, seem to be in some doubt, as an examination of multiple weights given for many detainees show wild swings in weight measurements, sometimes within one or two days, that do not seem physiologically possible.

[58] See URL: https://file.wikileaks.org/file/gitmo-sop-2003-2004.html, also https://.org/wiki/Camp_Delta_Standard_Operating_Procedure_(2004)

[59] See Chapter 8, pp. 56-63, "Detainee Management Rules" in the Camp Delta SOP. http://www1.umn.edu/humanrts/OathBetrayed/sop_2004.pdf

[60] Amnesty International, USA: Cruel and Inhuman: Conditions of isolation for detainees at Guantánamo Bay, April 2007, p. 5, URL: https://www.amnesty.ie/sites/default/files/report/2010/04/guantanamo%20conditions%20main%20text-FINAL.pdf (accessed June 12, 2016)

[61] Ibid. p. 7

[62] Carol Rosenberg, "Guantánamo downsizes by closing one prison, cutting 400 troops," Miami Herald, September 7, 2016,

URL: http://www.miamiherald.com/news/nation-world/world/americas/guantanamo/article100496357.html (accessed September 11, 2016)

[63] Kathleen T. Rhem, "Automated System Helps Guantanamo Guards Track Detainees," February 17, 2005, American Forces Press Service, URL: http://archive.defense.gov/news/newsarticle.aspx?id=25866

[64] Reference links at footnotes 58 and 59.

[65] Another copy of the autopsy report can be accessed at "The Torture Database," URL: https://www.thetorturedatabase.org/document/autopsy-report-muhammad-ahmad-al-hanashi-guantanamo-bay-cuba-june-23-2009-suicide-death

Of some interest is the way the autopsy report was publicly released. It was included in a 1,100-plus-page release of documents declassified by the DoD in 2011 in response to an American Civil Liberties Union Freedom of Information Act (FOIA) lawsuit. Hanashi's autopsy, and another autopsy, that of Abdul Rahman Al Amri, found dead in his cell in May 2007, went unexamined, until I noticed them and published an analysis in a February 29, 2012 article at the online website Truthout. See "Recently Released Autopsy Reports Heighten Guantanamo 'Suicides' Mystery," URL: http://www.truth-out.org/news/item/6981:recently-released-autopsy-reports-heighten-guantanamo-suicides-mystery

[66] Carol Rosenberg, "Captives Rigged Nooses", URL: http://www.miamiherald.com/news/nation-world/world/americas/guantanamo/article1928451.html (accessed August 26, 2016)

[67] Jane Sutton, "Mystery underwear stymies Guantanamo investigators," October 18, 2007, Reuters, URL: http://www.reuters.com/article/2007/10/18/us-bg-guantanamo-underwear-idUSNASUA170120071018 (accessed September 11, 2016)

[68] Robert Verkaik, "The case of the Guantanamo lawyer, the detainees and the illegal pairs of pants," UK Independent, September 13, 2007, URL:

http://www.independent.co.uk/news/world/americas/the-case-of-the-guantanamo-lawyer-the-detainees-and-the-illegal-pairs-of-pants-402338.html (accessed August 28, 2016)

[69] Carol Rosenberg, "Captives Rig Nooses," Miami Herald, October 17, 2007, URL: http://www.miamiherald.com/news/nation-world/world/americas/guantanamo/article1928451.html (accessed August 26, 2016)

[70] See page 1 of Al Hanashi documents, Part 6, "Results of Review of Evidence and Command Materials," NCIS Investigative Action, June 4, 2009, URL: http://GuantanamoTruth.com

[71] April 1, 2009, and undated, transcripts of writings of Mohammed Al Hanashi. See Al Hanashi documents, Part 2, pp. 2-3, URL: http://GuantanamoTruth.com

[72] Robert Mackey, "Miss Universe Visits Guantánamo Bay," New York Times, March 30, 2009, URL: http://thelede.blogs.nytimes.com/2009/03/30/miss-universe-visits-guantanamo/?hp&_r=0 (accessed September 5, 2009)

[73] See Stuart Grassian, "Psychiatric Effects of Solitary Confinement," Washington University Journal of Law & Policy, vol. 22, January 2006, URL: http://openscholarship.wustl.edu/cgi/viewcontent.cgi?article=1362&context=law_journal_law_policy

[74] Binyam Mohamed, "Was detainee's death a suicide?" Miami Herald, June 11, 2009, URL: http://humanrights.ucdavis.edu/projects/the-guantanamo-testimonials-project/testimonies/prisoner-testimonies/was-detainee2019s-death-a-suicide

[75] "SUBJECT: Recommendation for Continued Detention Under DoD Control (CD) for Guantanamo Detainee, ISN US9YM-000078DP," June 10, 2008, published by Wikileaks, URL: https://wikileaks.org/gitmo/prisoner/78.html (accessed August 3, 2016)

[76] Andy Worthington, "Yemeni Prisoner Muhammad Salih Dies At Guantánamo," June 2, 2009, URL:

http://www.andyworthington.co.uk/2009/06/02/yemeni-prisoner-muhammad-salih-dies-at-guantanamo/ (accessed August 3, 2016)

[77] This section of the background of Mohammad Al Hanashi draws heavily on my previously published article at Truthout, "Murder at Guantanamo?" November 20, 2009, URL: http://truth-out.org/archive/component/k2/item/86847:murder-at-guantanamo (accessed August 3, 2009)

[78] Combatant Status Review Tribunal Transcripts for Mohammad Salih Al Hanashi, undated, http://projects.nytimes.com/guantanamo/detainees/78-mohammad-ahmed-abdullah-saleh-al-hanashi/documents/4 (accessed August 3, 2016)

[79] James Risen, "U.S. Inaction Seen After Taliban P.O.W.'s Died," New York Times, July 10, 2009, URL: http://www.nytimes.com/2009/07/11/world/asia/11afghan.html?_r=1 (accessed August 3, 2016).

[80] Naomi Wolf, "What Happened to Mohamed al-Hanashi?" Project Syndicate, August 31, 2009, URL: https://www.project-syndicate.org/commentary/what-happened-to-mohamed-al-hanashi?barrier=true (accessed August 3, 2016).

[81] Fiza Asar, "Guantanamo Suicide Raises Questions: Binyam Claims Mohammad Abdullah Saleh Was Killed," Suite101.com, July 30, 2009, URL: http://web.archive.org/web/20100206005834/http://international-human-rights.suite101.com/article.cfm/guantanamo_suicide_raises_questions (accessed August 3, 2016).

[82] Michael Isikoff, "Did High-Value Detainee Commit Suicide in Libya?", Newsweek, May 11, 2009, URL: http://www.newsweek.com/did-high-value-detainee-commit-suicide-libya-79805 (accessed September 5, 2016).

[83] "Libya/US: Investigate Death of Former CIA Prisoner," Human Rights Watch, May 11, 2009, URL: https://www.hrw.org/news/2009/05/11/libya/us-investigate-death-former-cia-prisoner (accessed September 5, 2016).

[84] See Part 7, page 4, "Results Death Scene Examination," June 4, 2009, NCIS records on Mohammed Al Hanashi at http://www.guantanamotruth.com

[85] Neil A. Lewis, "Red Cross Finds Detainee Abuse in Guantánamo," New York Times, November 30, 2004, URL: http://www.nytimes.com/2004/11/30/politics/red-cross-finds-detainee-abuse-in-guantanamo.html?_r=0 (accessed September 11, 2016).

[86] June 4, 2009 "Statement" of the Chief of Behavioral Health Services for JTF GTMO. See Al Hanashi documents, Part 8, pp. 16-18, URL: http://GuantanamoTruth.com

[87] URL: https://wikileaks.org/gitmo/prisoner/199.html (accessed July 31, 2016)

[88] "Summarized Unsworn Detainee Statement" of ISN #199, Undated, The Guantanamo Testimonials Project, UC Davis, URL: http://humanrights.ucdavis.edu/projects/the-guantanamo-testimonials-project/testimonies/testimonies-of-the-defense-department/csrts-1/csrt_statement_199.pdf (accessed July 31, 2016)

[89] "SUBJECT: Recommendation for Continued Detention Under DoD Control (CD) for Guantanamo Detainee, ISN US9SA-000264DP (S)," March 2, 2006, published by Wikileaks, URL: https://commons.wikimedia.org/wiki/File:ISN_264%27s_Guantanamo_detainee_assessment.pdf (accessed August 3, 2016)

[90] See URL of released document: https://web.archive.org/web/20090125034041/http://www.dod.mil/pubs/foi/detainees/measurements/ISN_186-ISN_251.pdf (accessed August 3, 2016)

[91] David Hicks, Guantanamo: My Story, Random House, 2012, p. 219.

[92] "Guantanamo 'suicide' inmate named," BBC News, June 1, 2007, URL: http://news.bbc.co.uk/2/hi/americas/6710505.stm (accessed July 31, 2016) - Interestingly, at the same time, a Washington Post article on Al Amri's death portrayed the Camp 5 facility only as "a modern building in which detainees have

their own small cells." See Josh White, "Detainee Found Dead Trained With U.S. Forces," Washington Post, June 1, 2007, URL: http://www.washingtonpost.com/wp-dyn/content/article/2007/05/31/AR2007053100294.html?hpid=moreheadlines (accessed July 31, 2016).

[93] Carol Rosenberg, *op. cit.* (footnote 69)

[94] Candace Gorman, "Suicide and Spin Doctors," In These Times, October 17, 2007, URL: http://inthesetimes.com/article/3374/suicide_and_spin_doctors (accessed August 28, 2016)

[95] Ben Fox, "Saudi Warned Before Suicide That Some at Guantanamo 'Would Rather Die,'" Associated Press, September 20, 2007, archived at Cageprisoners website, URL: http://old.cageprisoners.com/articles.php?id=21782 (accessed August 3, 2016)

[96] Summary of Evidence, Department of Defense Office for the Administrative Review of the Detention of Enemy Combatants, re Al Amri, Abdul Rahman Ma Ath Thafir, October 6, 2005, URL: https://assets.documentcloud.org/documents/76277/isn-199-abdul-rahman-maath-thafir-al-amri.pdf (accessed August 3, 2016)

[97] Ojeda, *op. cit.* (footnote 54)

[98] Jeffrey Kaye, "NCIS Hid Medical Evidence About Guantanamo Suicides," The Dissenter/Shadowproof, June 4, 2014, URL: https://shadowproof.com/2014/06/03/new-report-ncis-hid-medical-evidence-about-guantanamo-suicides/ (accessed September 10, 2016). See also Mark Denbeaux, et al., Uncovering the Cover Ups: Death in Camp Delta, Seton Hall Public Law Research Paper No. 2437423, May 2014, URL: http://papers.ssrn.com/sol3/papers.cfm?abstract_id=2437423

[99] See URL: http://humanrights.ucdavis.edu/projects/the-guantanamo-testimonials-project/testimonies/testimonies-of-standard-operating-procedures/camp_delta_sop_2004.pdf

[100] For text of letter, see URL: https://www.documentcloud.org/documents/536275-adnan-latifs-may-28-2010-letter-to-attorneys.html. Also see Jason

Leopold and Jeffrey Kaye, "Latif Letter About Guantanamo Speaks From the Grave: 'I Am Being Pushed Toward Death Every Moment'", December 10, 2012, Truthout, URL: http://www.truth-out.org/news/item/13234-latif-letter-about-guantanamo-speaks-from-the-grave-i-am-being-pushed-toward-death-every-moment

[101] Jeffrey Kaye, "Recently Released Autopsy Reports Heighten Guantanamo "Suicides" Mystery", Truthout, February 29, 2012, URL: http://www.truth-out.org/news/item/6981:recently-released-autopsy-reports-heighten-guantanamo-suicides-mystery (accessed June 16, 2016)

[102] "Common Means of Suicide," no date, URL: http://dmmoyle.com/simeans.htm (accessed August 17, 2016)

[103] Al Amri's toxicology report at URL: https://www.documentcloud.org/documents/2695560-FOIA-Al-Amri-Toxicology-Report.html

[104] Al Amri autopsy report at URL: https://www.documentcloud.org/documents/2680677-Autopsy-Report-Al-Amri-Aka-Al-Umari-ISN-199.html

[105] Jason Leopold and Jeffrey Kaye, "EXCLUSIVE: Controversial Drug Given to All Guantanamo Detainees Akin to "Pharmacologic Waterboarding" Truthout, December 1, 2010, URL: http://www.truth-out.org/news/item/253:exclusive-controversial-drug-given-to-all-guantanamo-detainees-akin-to-pharmacologic-waterboarding (accessed August 17, 2016)

[106] Jason Leopold and Jeffrey Kaye, "Ex-Guantanamo Official Was Told Not to Discuss Policy Surrounding Antimalarial Drug Used on Detainees," Truthout, December 20, 2010, URL: http://www.truth-out.org/news/item/254:exguantanamo-official-was-told-not-to-discuss-policy-surrounding-antimalarial-drug-used-on-detainees (accessed August 17, 2016)

[107] Jeffrey Kaye, "A Guantanamo Connection? Documents Show CIA Stockpiled Antimalaria Drugs as 'Incapacitating Agents,'" Truthout, June 6, 2012, URL: http://www.truth-out.org/news/item/9601-a-guantanamo-connection-documents-show-cia-stockpiled-antimalaria-drugs-as-incapacitating-agents (accessed August 17, 2016)

[108] Jason Leopold, "Widespread Breakdown of Safeguards at Gitmo," Al Jazeera, July 3, 2013, URL: http://www.aljazeera.com/humanrights/2013/07/20137324426228887.html (accessed August 17, 2016)

[109] Jeffrey Kaye, "New DoD Report Details Nightmare Leading to Gitmo Detainee's Death," Shadowproof, June 29, 2013, URL: https://shadowproof.com/2013/06/29/new-dod-report-details-nightmare-leading-to-gitmo-detainees-death/ (accessed August 17, 2016)

[110] Former detainee David Hicks discusses that fact in his book on his experiences, Guantanamo, My Journey. An extraordinary memoir, it was published by Random House in Australia in 2012, but it was never put on sale in the United States, and used copies are rare in this country.

[111] See 25Jun07 Interim Report of Investigation (ROI) at Al Amri NCIS notes, PDF 3 at www.GuantanamoTruth.com

[112] Samir Al-Saadi, "Deceased Guantanamo Detainee 'Suffered' in Guantanamo," June 1, 2007, Arab News (reprinted at Cageprisoners.com), URL: http://old.cageprisoners.com/articles.php?id=20548

[113] Raid Qusti & Galal Fakkar, "Gitmo Suicide: Al-Amri Relatives Suspect Foul Play," Arab News, June 6, 2007, URL: http://web.archive.org/web/20120306171012/http://archive.arabnews.com/?page=1&section=0&article=97140&d=6&m=6&y=2007 (accessed August 17, 2016)

[114] This chapter is adapted with some changes from two original, earlier publications: Jeffrey Kaye, "New DoD Report Details Nightmare Leading to Gitmo Detainee's Death," The Dissenter (later renamed Shadowproof), June 29, 2013, URL: https://shadowproof.com/2013/06/29/new-dod-report-details-nightmare-leading-to-gitmo-detainees-death/; and Jeffrey Kaye, "Southcom Commander Spins Latif Death Investigation to Justify Groin Searches," The Dissenter (Shadowproof), July 18, 2013, URL: https://shadowproof.com/2013/07/18/southcom-commander-spins-latif-death-investigation-to-justify-groin-searches/

[115] Memorandum, "10 June 2008" to "Commander, United States Southern Command, 3511 NW 9lst Avenue, Miami, FL 33172," "SUBJECT: Recommendation for Transfer Out of DoD Control (TRO) for Guantanamo Detainee, ISN US9YM-000156DP (S)." URL: https://wikileaks.org/gitmo/prisoner/156.html (accessed August 22, 2016)

[116] Jonathan Hafetz, Mark P. Denbeaux, The Guantánamo Lawyers: Inside a Prison Outside the Law, NYU Press, 2011, p. 158.

[117] Jeffrey Kaye, "Gitmo Detainee's Body Returned To Yemen, New Details On His Death Revealed," The Public Record, December 16, 2012, URL: http://pubrecord.org/world/10661/gitmo-detainees-returned-yemen/. See also, U.S. Southern Command Courtesy Story, "Latif Remains Repatriated to Yemen," December 15, 2016, URL: https://www.dvidshub.net/news/99360/latif-remains-repatriated-yemen (accessed August 20, 2017)

[118] Jeffrey Kaye and Jason Leopold, "EXCLUSIVE: DoD Report Reveals Some Detainees Interrogated While Drugged, Others "Chemically Restrained," Truthout, July 11, 2012, URL: http://www.truth-out.org/news/item/10248-exclusive-department-of-defense-declassifies-report-on-alleged-drugging-of-detainees (accessed August 20, 2012)

[119] Jason Leopold, "A Guantanamo Prisoner Is Buried as New Details About His Death Begin to Surface," Truthout, January 11, 2013, URL: http://www.truth-out.org/news/item/13818-guantanamo-prisoner-buried-new-details-death-surface (accessed August 20, 2016)

[120] Andy Worthington, "EXCLUSIVE: The Last Days in the Life of Adnan Latif, Who Died in Guantánamo Last Year," July 19, 2013, URL: http://www.andyworthington.co.uk/2013/07/19/exclusive-the-last-days-in-the-life-of-adnan-latif-who-died-in-guantanamo-last-year/ (accessed August 21, 2016)

[121] Jason Leopold, "Widespread Breakdown of Safeguards at Gitmo," Al Jazeera, July 13, 2013, URL:

http://www.aljazeera.com/humanrights/2013/07/20137324426228887.html (accessed September 4, 2016)

[122] Herman Schwartz, "Imprisonment without end at Gitmo," Politico, September 21, 2012, URL: http://www.politico.com/story/2012/09/imprisonment-without-end-at-gitmo-081515 (accessed August 20, 2016)

[123] Jeffrey Kaye, "Recently Released Autopsy Reports Heighten Guantanamo "Suicides" Mystery", Truthout, February 29, 2012, URL: http://www.truth-out.org/news/item/6981:recently-released-autopsy-reports-heighten-guantanamo-suicides-mystery (accessed June 16, 2016)

[124] Jeffrey Kaye, "Citing Truthout Report, UN Special Rapporteur 'Looking Into' Guantanamo 'Suicides,'" Truthout, March 27, 2012, URL: http://www.truth-out.org/news/item/8112-citing-truthout-report-un-special-rapporteur-looking-into-guantanamo-suicides (accessed June 16, 2016)

[125] Jonathan Horowitz, Counterterrorism and Human Rights Abuses in Kenya and Uganda: The World Cup Bombing and Beyond, Open Society Foundations, 2013, URL: https://www.opensocietyfoundations.org/sites/default/files/counterterrorism-human-rights-abuses-kenya-uganda-20130403.pdf (accessed August 21, 2016)

[126] See Anna Louise Sussman, "Naji Hamdan's Nightmare," The Nation, March 4, 2010, URL: https://www.thenation.com/article/naji-hamdans-nightmare/; Mark Mazzetti, "Detained American Says He Was Beaten in Kuwait," New York Times, January 5, 2011, URL: http://www.nytimes.com/2011/01/06/world/middleeast/06detain.html; Nick Baumann, "American Muslim Alleges FBI Had a Hand in His Torture (Updated with Video), Mother Jones, April 17, 2012, URL: http://www.motherjones.com/politics/2012/04/yonas-fikre-american-proxy-detention-tortured-uae; Jeremy Scahill, "The CIA's Secret Sites in Somalia," The Nation, December 10, 2014, URL: https://www.thenation.com/article/cias-secret-sites-somalia/ (accessed August 21, 2016)

[127] Jeffrey Kaye, "UN Review Cites Torture & 'Ill Treatment' in US Army Field Manual's Appendix M," Shadowproof, November 28, 2014, URL: https://shadowproof.com/2014/11/28/un-review-cites-torture-ill-treatment-in-u-s-army-field-manuals-appendix-m/ (accessed August 21, 2016)

[128] See Beth Van Schaack, "The Torture Convention & Appendix M of the Army Field Manual on Interrogations," Just Security, December 5, 2014, URL: https://www.justsecurity.org/18043/torture-convention-appendix-army-field-manual-interrogations/; Deb Riechmann, "A little-known appendix to US interrogations manual still allows sleep deprivation, other sensory techniques that some say amount to torture," US News and World Report, March 11, 2016, URL: http://www.usnews.com/news/politics/articles/2016-03-11/torture-is-illegal-but-theres-the-issue-of-appendix-m; Ali Watkins and Aram Roston, "Obama's Interrogation Methods," Buzzfeed News, July 13, 2016, URL: https://www.buzzfeed.com/alimwatkins/documents-raise-disturbing-questions-about-detainee-abuse-un (accessed August 21, 2016)

[129] Steven H. Miles, "Medical Investigations of Homicides of Prisoners of War in Iraq and Afghanistan," Medscape General Medicine, 2005; 7(3): 4. Published online 2005 Jul 5. URL: http://www.ncbi.nlm.nih.gov/pmc/articles/PMC1681676/ (accessed August 22, 2016)

[130] M. G. Bloche and J. H. Marks, "When doctors go to war," New England Journal of Medicine, 2005; 352:3–6.

[131] Camp Delta Standard Operating Procedures (SOP), March 28, 2003, Headquarters, Joint Task Force Guantanamo, URL: http://www1.umn.edu/humanrts/OathBetrayed/SOP 1-238.pdf (accessed August 22, 2016)

[132] See Matt Stroud, "A Death in Solitary: Did Corrections Officers Help an Inmate Kill Himself?" Alternet, August 13, 2010, URL: http://www.alternet.org/story/147840/a_death_in_solitary%3A_

did_corrections_officers_help_an_inmate_kill_himself (accessed August 21, 2016)

[133] "State to investigate allegations about Dallas prison guards," The Times Leader, September 11, 2009, URL: http://archives.timesleader.com/2009_19/2009_09_11_State_to_investigate_allegations_about_Dallas_prison_guards_-news.html (accessed August 21, 2016)

[134] See http://www.medword.com/griefEF.html (accessed August 21, 2016)

[135] Scott Shane, "China Inspired Interrogations at Guantánamo," New York Times, July 2, 2008, URL: http://www.nytimes.com/2008/07/02/us/02detain.html?_r=0 (accessed September 4, 2016). For Biderman's chart itself, see Albert D. Biderman, "Communist Attempts to Elicit False Confessions from Air Force Prisoners of War," Bulletin of the New York Academy of Medicine, Vol. 33 (9), September 1957, pp. 616–625, URL: http://graphics8.nytimes.com/packages/pdf/national/20080702_1957.pdf (accessed September 4, 2016, see page 4 of PDF). For a critical view of the Biderman document, see Jeff Kaye, "The Truth About False Confessions," Shadowproof, June 25, 2009, URL: https://shadowproof.com/2009/06/25/the-truth-about-false-confessions/ (accessed September 4, 2016).

[136] See Valtin (aka Jeffrey Kaye), "New Documents Show U.S. Torture Was Planned Long Ago," Daily Kos, February 9, 2007, URL: https://valtinsblog.blogspot.com/2007/03/new-documents-show-us-torture-was.html (accessed September 4, 2016)

[137] Greg Miller, "How a modest contract for 'applied research' morphed into the CIA's brutal interrogation program," Washington Post, July 13, 2013, URL: https://www.washingtonpost.com/news/checkpoint/wp/2016/07/13/how-a-modest-contract-for-applied-research-morphed-into-the-cias-brutal-interrogation-program/. See also the text of the contracts themselves. The Washington Post link for the contracts was broken the day I last checked, but you can also read them at URL: https://www.documentcloud.org/documents/2992829-Read-the-contracts-for-James-Mitchell.html (accessed September 4, 2016).

[138] Jeffrey S. Kaye, "Isolation, Sensory Deprivation, and Sensory Overload: History, Research, and Interrogation Policy, from the 1950s to the Present Day," Guild Practitioner, Vol. 66, No. 1, Spring 2009, pp. 2-17 (URL: http://www.nlg.org/resource/nlg-review/volume-66-no-1 (accessed September 11, 2016)

[139] Jeffrey Kaye, "CIA declassifies new portions of Cold War-era interrogation manual," Muckrock, April 8, 2014, URL: https://www.muckrock.com/news/archives/2014/apr/08/cia-declassifies-additional-portions-kubark-interr/ (accessed September 11, 2016)

Made in the USA
Lexington, KY
21 February 2017